ORIGAMI JEWELLERY

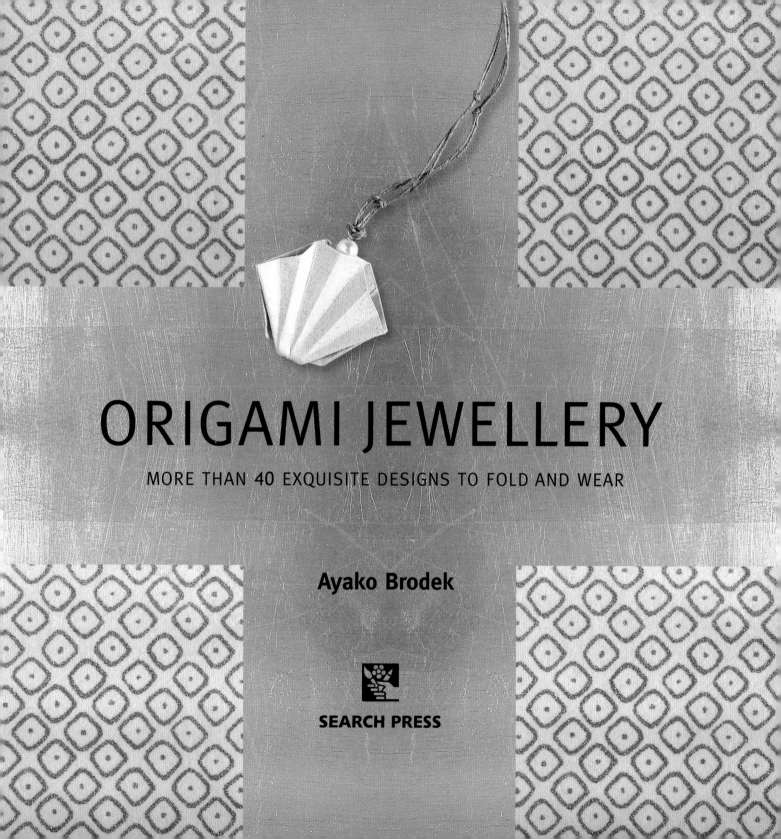

ORIGAMI JEWELLERY

MORE THAN 40 EXQUISITE DESIGNS TO FOLD AND WEAR

Ayako Brodek

SEARCH PRESS

A QUARTO BOOK

Published in 2007 by Search Press Ltd
Wellwood
North Farm Road
Tunbridge Wells
Kent TN2 3DR
United Kingdom

ISBN-13: 978 1 84448 287 0
ISBN-10: 1 84448 287 1

A catalogue record for this book is available from the
British Library

Conceived, designed and produced by
Quarto Publishing plc
The Old Brewery
6 Blundell Street
London N7 9BH

QUA: ORJ

Project editors: **Mary Groom** & **Katie Hallam**
Art editor and designer: **Elizabeth Healey**
Managing art editor: **Anna Plucinska**
Assistant art director: **Caroline Guest**
Copy editor: **Bridget Jones**
Photographer: **Phil Wilkins**
Illustrator: **Stephen Dew**
Indexer: **Joan Dearnley**

Art director: **Moira Clinch**
Publisher: **Paul Carslake**

Colour separation by Provision PTE, Ltd., Singapore
Printed by SNP Leefung Printers Ltd, China

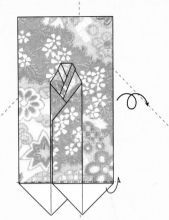

CONTENTS

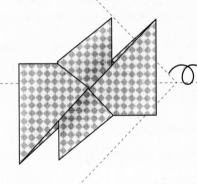

CONTINUED ON NEXT PAGE

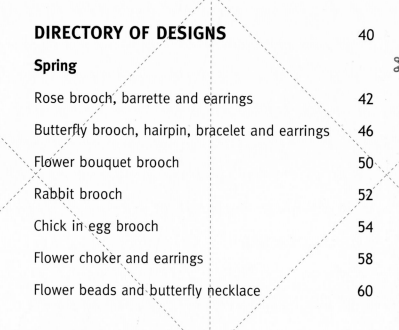

DIRECTORY OF DESIGNS

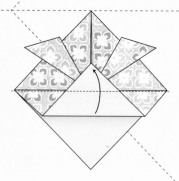

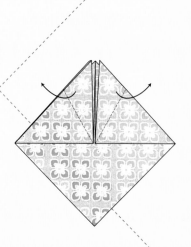

Winter

Japanese

INTRODUCTION

My love of origami began when I was a little girl. On long ferryboat rides to my grandparents' house, my mother would chase away my boredom by making origami cranes and boats from sweet wrappers. I never stopped folding.

When an opportunity came to teach origami at my sons' school, I couldn't pass up the chance to share this wonderful art with children. Preparing for the class, I folded origami cranes, remembering my mother's tiny sweet-wrapper ones. I thought it might be cute to attach earring findings and wear them to class. That was the first origami jewellery I made.

The many compliments on the earrings from the children and parents sparked my exploration of wearable origami. I became obsessed with finding designs, materials and finishing techniques that can be worn by any age.

This book is a compilation of my favourite pieces, along with the necessary guidance and knowledge to make origami jewellery you'll love.

About this book

Getting started
Everything you need to begin origami jewellery-making is covered in the front section. Familiarize yourself with the key techniques and equipment needed to complete the projects in the rest of the book.

The projects
The main projects are categorized by season, with a special Japanese section toward the back of the book. Detailed artwork will guide you step by step through the folding and assembling processes, and full-colour photography shows the stunning end result.

Indication of the skill level required, with one being easy; three more challenging

Comprehensive list of all the materials and tools needed

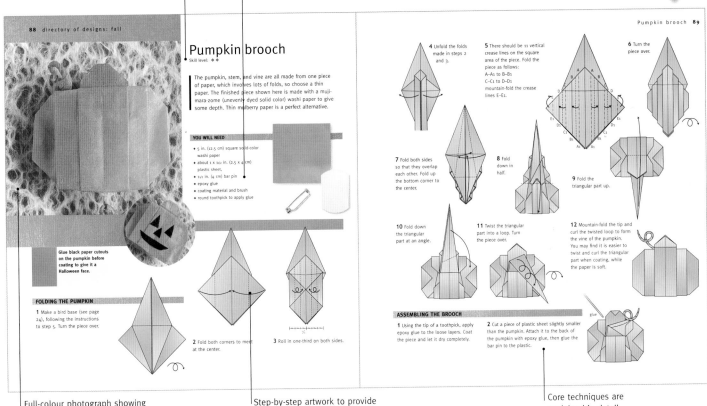

88   directory of designs: fall

Pumpkin brooch
Skill level: ❖ ❖

The pumpkin, stem, and vine are all made from one piece of paper, which involves lots of folds, so choose a thin paper. The finished piece shown here is made with a muji-mara-zome (unevenly dyed solid color) washi paper to give some depth. Thin mulberry paper is a perfect alternative.

YOU WILL NEED
- 5 in. (12.5 cm) square solid-color washi paper
- about 1 x 1½ in. (2.5 x 4 cm) plastic sheet
- 1½ in. (4 cm) bar pin
- epoxy glue
- coating material and brush
- round toothpick to apply glue

Glue black paper cutouts on the pumpkin before coating to give it a Halloween face.

FOLDING THE PUMPKIN

1 Make a bird base (see page 24), following the instructions to step 5. Turn the piece over.

2 Fold both corners to meet at the center.

3 Roll in one-third on both sides.

Pumpkin brooch   **89**

4 Unfold the folds made in steps 2 and 3.

5 There should be 11 vertical crease lines on the square area of the piece. Fold the piece as follows:
A–A₁ to B–B₁
C–C₁ to D–D₁
mountain-fold the crease lines E–E₁.

6 Turn the piece over.

7 Fold both sides so that they overlap each other. Fold up the bottom corner to the center.

8 Fold down in half.

9 Fold the triangular part up.

10 Fold down the triangular part at an angle.

11 Twist the triangular part into a loop. Turn the piece over.

12 Mountain-fold the tip and curl the twisted loop to form the vine of the pumpkin. You may find it is easier to twist and curl the triangular part when coating, while the paper is soft.

ASSEMBLING THE BROOCH

1 Using the tip of a toothpick, apply epoxy glue to the loose layers. Coat the piece and let it dry completely.

2 Cut a piece of plastic sheet slightly smaller than the pumpkin. Attach it to the back of the pumpkin with epoxy glue, then glue the bar pin to the plastic.

Full-colour photograph showing the finished jewellery

Step-by-step artwork to provide additional guidance

Core techniques are explained in detail

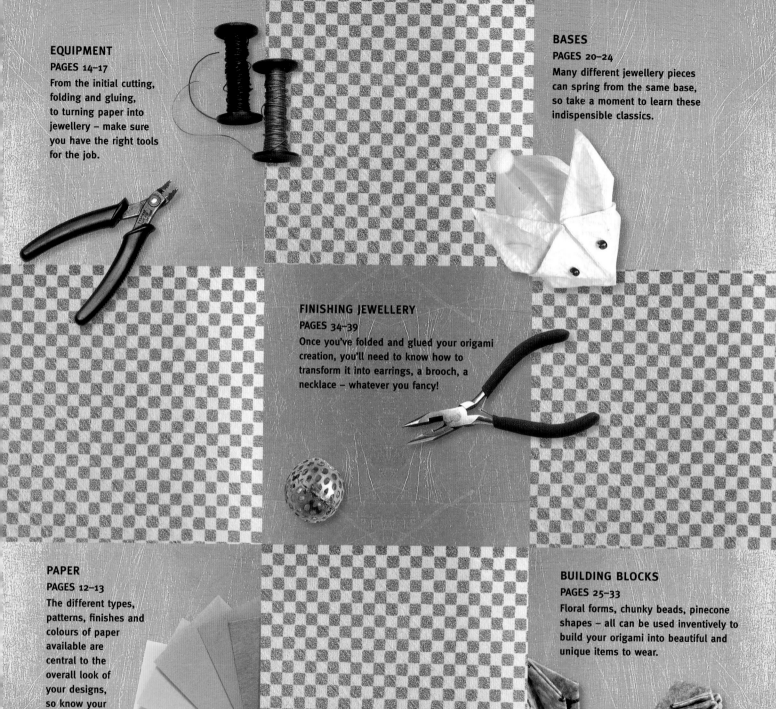

EQUIPMENT
PAGES 14–17
From the initial cutting, folding and gluing, to turning paper into jewellery – make sure you have the right tools for the job.

BASES
PAGES 20–24
Many different jewellery pieces can spring from the same base, so take a moment to learn these indispensible classics.

FINISHING JEWELLERY
PAGES 34–39
Once you've folded and glued your origami creation, you'll need to know how to transform it into earrings, a brooch, a necklace – whatever you fancy!

PAPER
PAGES 12–13
The different types, patterns, finishes and colours of paper available are central to the overall look of your designs, so know your options before you choose.

BUILDING BLOCKS
PAGES 25–33
Floral forms, chunky beads, pinecone shapes – all can be used inventively to build your origami into beautiful and unique items to wear.

BEING WELL EQUIPPED

WITH THE ESSENTIAL TOOLS

AND KNOWLEDGE ENSURES

YOU'LL ACHIEVE THE BEST

RESULTS IN YOUR ORIGAMI

JEWELLERY-MAKING.

TOOLS AND TECHNIQUES

SO FAMILIARIZE YOURSELF

WITH ALL YOU NEED TO KNOW

TO GET STARTED AND TO WORK

SUCCESSFULLY THROUGH THE

PROJECTS THAT FOLLOW.

Frog brooch and earrings, page 120

Choosing paper

Choosing the right paper is the key to creating origami jewellery that you will love to wear or give as gifts. Traditional or modern, subtle or vivid, elegant or funky – you can vary the look of the jewellery simply by choosing different paper. There are numerous types available, and while the projects in this book give suggested papers for each project, don't let that limit the possibilities – go ahead and experiment.

These pages explain the characteristics and properties of the papers that can be used for origami jewellery. The qualities of each are demonstrated using a traditional frog brooch design. Some are easy to fold, some are a little trickier. Durability varies with paper type, and some are more suitable for coating than others.

These are all factors to consider when selecting paper for your project.

Colour choices
The frog is a powerful symbol of good fortune in Japan. Stick with tradition and give yours a gorgeous green theme.

Washi

Although you can experiment with lots of different types of paper, traditional Japanese paper, called "washi" is the best choice for origami jewellery. It is beautiful, durable, soft, easy to fold and suitable for both large and small pieces. The washi manufacturing process leaves the paper fibres long and randomly positioned, giving it incredible strength and no grain. The lack of grain means you can make clean folds in any direction, in any size, without ripping or tearing. Washi is also highly absorbent, so the coating material soaks through the entire paper, resulting in outstanding durability for the finished piece.

Many different types of washi are produced, for many different purposes. Two good choices for origami jewellery are Yuzen washi and Mujizome washi. Although washi is wonderful, it is not always easily available at local shops, and can be more expensive than other kinds of paper.

Different effects
Choose from pretty plain or patterned papers to make these delightful earrings. The examples shown here demonstrate the wide range of effects that can be achieved.

Yuzen washi
Yuzen washi is great for origami jewellery. "Yuzen" refers to traditional Japanese textile designs used for kimonos. These designs are silkscreened onto washi sheets, and there are endless exquisite designs and colours to choose from.

Origami paper

Specifically designed for origami folding, packages of these bright, single-colour sheets of square paper are easily available. Although not as durable as washi, origami paper can work well for small items such as earrings, and is perfect for practising folding.

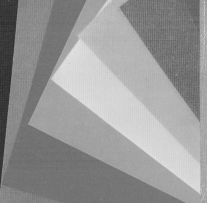

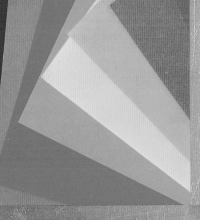

Photocopy paper

Produced in white and many wonderful colours, this inexpensive paper is easily available at any stationery shop. Since the entire sheet is dyed, no white crease lines will show at folds. It may not withstand repeated folding without tearing when you are working on a small piece, yet it can work well with large or simple pieces.

Foil and opalescent origami paper

Also made specifically for origami folding, foil and opalescent origami paper is easy to fold and gives jewellery a unique bright and shiny appearance. It is not suitable for coating, but the shiny surface provides some durability.

Scrapbook paper

Scrapbook paper is available in a huge range of irresistible prints. Since it is not designed for folding, many papers are too thick or textured for small or complicated pieces. However, if you find a design you can't resist, try it for large or simple pieces. White crease lines may become visible, so avoid dark colours.

Mujizome washi

Mujizome ("no-pattern dye") washi is dyed with a single solid colour, and is available in both subtle and rich shades. Mujizome washi has a felt-like texture. The coating process can be a little tricky, since uneven coating leaves marks.

Japanese folk-art pattern origami paper

Printed with Yuzen kimono and traditional folk-art designs, this paper is thicker, stronger and softer than regular origami paper. Durable enough for larger pieces, its thickness can make folding smaller items more challenging, but it can be an inexpensive and readily available choice of paper.

Equipment

It may be true that, in addition to paper, your fingers are the only essential equipment for origami; however, when you want to create pieces to wear and enjoy for years, you need a few more items to achieve a good finish. This section is an overview of the helpful and essential tools and materials needed to create beautiful, durable and wearable origami jewellery.

Cutting

The key to perfect folding is precise cutting. There are several ways to achieve this: use a craft knife, cutting mat and ruler; draw lines on the back of paper and cut along these with scissors; use a paper cutter or trimmer. The choice depends on the tools you have and the method you prefer. When cutting, be careful not to damage your most important tools – your fingers!

Craft knife
A sharp blade is essential to cut a clean edge.

Cutting mat
A mat with a grid is helpful to measure right angles.

Ruler
Choose a safety ruler with non-slip backing and a barrier along one edge to protect your fingers. It can be used for measuring and as a straight edge. Plastic or wood rulers are not recommended as a guide for cutting with a craft knife.

Protractor
Make a perfect right angle when marking paper.

Pencil
Use to draw cutting lines on the back of paper.

Scissors
Long, sharp blades are ideal for cutting large pieces of paper. For small pieces, slitting, or trimming, a pair of embroidery scissors with short and pointed blades works well.

Paper cutter
Designed to cut through one sheet or a large stack, giving clean, straight edges. It has a long blade with a handle attached to a steady base. The face of the base usually has a grid on it and a ruler near the top.

Paper trimmer
Cuts paper accurately, quickly, easily and safely. It has a rotary blade mounted on a sliding shuttle attached to a rail.

Folding

You may be comfortable using your fingers, but there are some tools that help to achieve firm and sharp folds.

Bone folder

Use this to make crisp, firm creases and to smooth freshly glued surfaces.

Round toothpick

This is useful for many fiddly techniques, such as reaching into small corners, opening up pockets and reshaping pleats.

Durability

The best coating material to use is a satin-finish, water-based polyurethane, which can be found at craft shops that carry découpage supplies. The polyurethane soaks through the paper and hardens entire layers giving durability, while maintaining the warmth and flexibility of paper. Although it can be cleaned up with soap and water, once dried, the polyurethane makes the piece water-resistant. You will also need a variety of other items.

Small paint brush

For applying coating materials.

Small plastic or glass container

Something to hold a working amount of coating material.

Epoxy glue

Select one-part epoxy glue that dries like clear rubber and is acid-free when cured. "One-part" means the product is ready to use straight from the tube and you do not have to mix two substances to activate the glue. This craft adhesive is available at craft shops. Super-glue is not recommended because it is brittle when dry and shatters like glass.

Glue stick

Any glue stick that dries clear is suitable. Acid-free, extra-strength sticks made specifically for craft work are best.

Round toothpick

Useful for applying glue to small areas or into hard-to-reach areas.

Polyester stuffing

For padding areas to make pieces sturdy.

Wax paper or other non-stick surface

Place pieces on a non-stick surface while they dry.

Clothes-pegs

These are useful for holding glued layers together until dry.

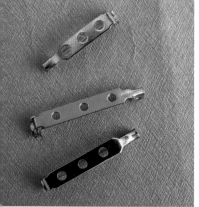

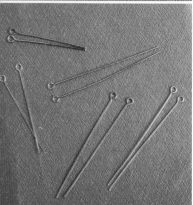

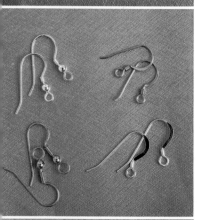

Finishing: jewellery findings

These transform your origami creation into jewellery. Each project has a list of items needed to complete the piece. You will find them at craft and beading shops, usually in a choice of 14 karat, base metal, gold-filled or sterling silver.

Bar pin
A pin with a bail, or ring, allows a brooch to be worn as a pendant.

Other pins
There are various other pins for different types of jewellery, including a tie tack and clutch, kilt pin, hairpin, barrette and stickpin.

Clasp, jump ring, split ring, connector, end bar, crimping bead, clear nail polish
To finish the ends of necklaces and bracelets.

Earring findings
Fish-hooks, earring posts and ear nuts are all used to finish earrings.

Head pin and eye pin
To connect or link origami pieces.

Plastic sheet or disc
This is used as backing for attaching a bar pin. Any sturdy plastic sheet can be used, for example, disposable plastic containers or packaging. The ideal thickness is about that of a credit card, which is thick enough not to bend easily, but thin enough to be cut with scissors. Be sure to trim all sharp corners.

Beading thread, beading wire and chain
These are used to string beads or charms.

Leather cord, knotting cord, hemp and twin cord
Used to hang origami charms or as embellishments.

hemp

plastic sheet

beading wire

linen

leather thongs

Findings
(from top) bar pins, eye pins, fish-hook findings and head pins.

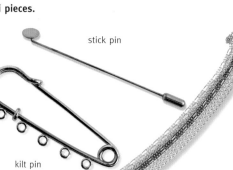

stick pin

kilt pin

chains

round-nose pliers

cutting pliers

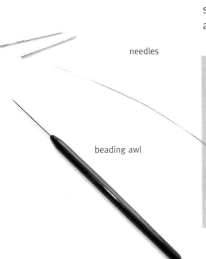

crimping pliers

needles

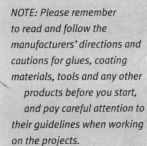

beading awl

Finishing tools

Round-nose pliers
To pinch and bend wire or pins.

Cutting pliers
To cut wire or pins.

Crimping pliers
To clamp crimp beads to wire or pins.

Beading needle or sewing needle
To thread beads or sew a bead onto a piece.

Beading awl
To pierce a hole. A sewing needle can be a substitute when piercing thin layers.

Embellishments
Be creative and use any embellishment you like – for example, ribbon, knotting cord, wire, pom-poms and other basics such as permanent marker pens.

Glass, wood, pearl, pewter, Swarovski, jade or seed – the variety of beads available is almost endless!

NOTE: Please remember to read and follow the manufacturers' directions and cautions for glues, coating materials, tools and any other products before you start, and pay careful attention to their guidelines when working on the projects.

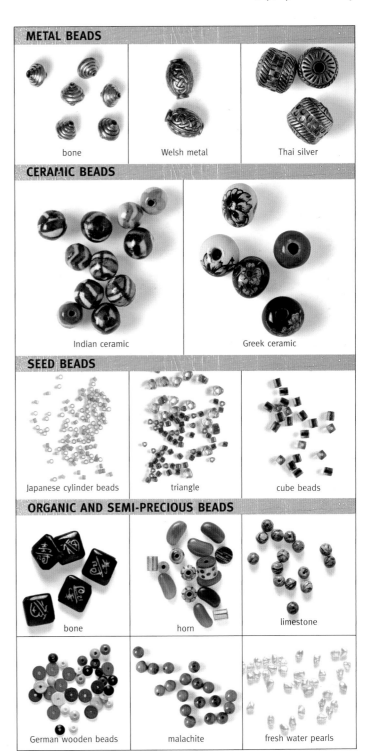

METAL BEADS

bone

Welsh metal

Thai silver

CERAMIC BEADS

Indian ceramic

Greek ceramic

SEED BEADS

Japanese cylinder beads

triangle

cube beads

ORGANIC AND SEMI-PRECIOUS BEADS

bone

horn

limestone

German wooden beads

malachite

fresh water pearls

Symbols

The instructions throughout this book are illustrated with clear diagrams, which make use of various symbols – such as arrows and lines – to show the direction of the fold, the type of fold, where to apply glue and any other essential information you may need to make the perfect origami jewellery project. Please use the following table as a reference to these symbols:

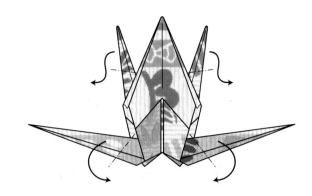

Fold	Fold behind	Fold and then unfold to make a crease line	Turn over
Rotate	Open up	Push or press	Valley fold
Mountain fold	Creased line	Equal distance	
Back or under side of paper (white side)	Top side of paper (coloured side)	Apply glue with a toothpick	

Traditional crane, page 108

Basic folds

Mastering folding is the key to creating beautiful origami jewellery. This section explains the basic origami symbols and folding techniques. If you are new to origami, the diagrams, with all the different arrows and lines, look confusing; however, once you learn the meaning of the symbols, the diagrams soon become clear, just like learning to read music. Before you start a project, practise with origami paper, using a larger sheet than required for the project.

VALLEY FOLD

The arrows indicate the folding direction.

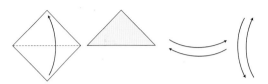
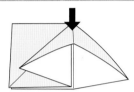
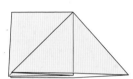

MOUNTAIN FOLD

To make a mountain fold, it is easier to turn the paper over, make a valley fold, and then turn the paper over again, than it is to lift the paper and fold it while holding it up.

OPEN AND FLATTEN OR SQUASH

Loosen the opening and separate the layers apart as you flatten them.

INSIDE REVERSE FOLD

Make a crease line where the reverse fold will be made, then fold the corner down between the layers.

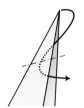
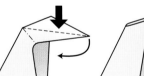

OUTSIDE REVERSE FOLD

Make a crease line where the outside reverse fold will be made, then open the paper, and flip the corner over.

HELPFUL HINTS

+ Work on a smooth, clean and solid surface.
+ Make folds as straight and exact as possible, and bring corners together exactly.
+ Crease folds firmly.
+ It is often easier to fold away from you – rotate the paper to facilitate folding.
+ Check the diagram for the next step to understand where the current step leads to. Better still, read through the whole project before you begin.
+ Most of all, enjoy!

Bases

Many origami designs begin with the same sequence of folding, which is called a base. The folding instructions of all the bases used in this book are explained on the following pages.

Heart earrings, page 106

PRELIMINARY BASE: METHOD A

1 Fold in half lengthways, then unfold. Fold in half widthways, then unfold.

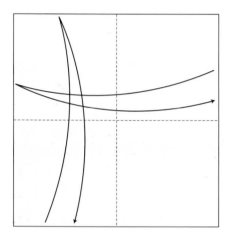

2 Fold in half diagonally.

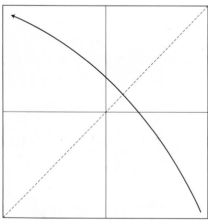

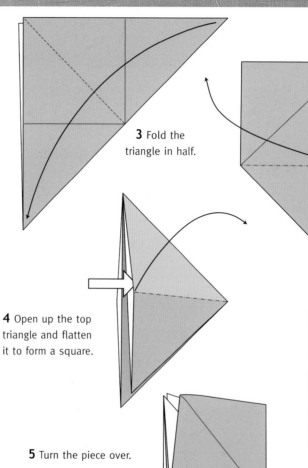

3 Fold the triangle in half.

4 Open up the top triangle and flatten it to form a square.

5 Turn the piece over.

6 Repeat step 4 on the other side to complete the preliminary base.

7 The finished preliminary base.

PRELIMINARY BASE: METHOD B

1 Fold in half widthways, then unfold.

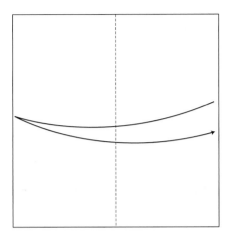

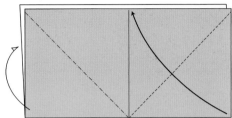

3 Fold the bottom right corner to the top centre, and mountain-fold the bottom left corner to the top centre.

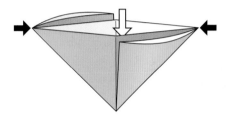

4 Open up the centre layers and press the sides together, then flatten the piece in half.

2 Fold in half lengthways from bottom to top.

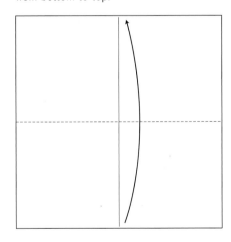

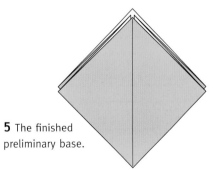

5 The finished preliminary base.

Flower beads, page 28

BLINTZ BASE

1 Fold in half lengthways then unfold. Fold in half widthways then unfold.

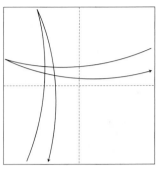

2 Fold the four corners to the centre.

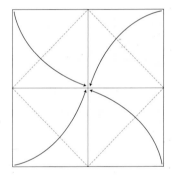

3 The finished blintz base.

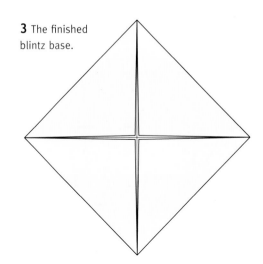

BALLOON BASE

1 Fold in half diagonally, then unfold. Fold in half diagonally in the other direction, then unfold.

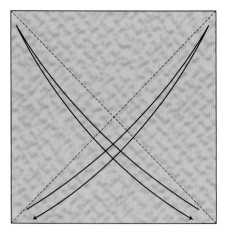

2 Fold in half lengthways.

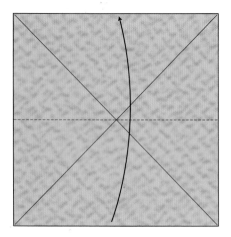

3 Fold in half widthways.

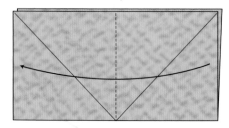

Rabbit brooch, page 52

4 Bring the corner of the top layer out to the side, and open up the square.

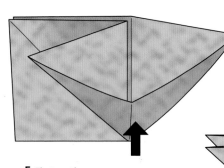

5 Flatten the open square to form a triangle.

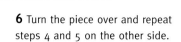

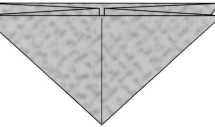

6 Turn the piece over and repeat steps 4 and 5 on the other side.

7 The finished balloon base.

BOAT BASE

1 Fold in half lengthways then unfold. Fold in half widthways then unfold. Turn the piece over.

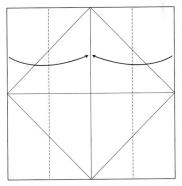

3 Fold both sides to meet at the centre crease.

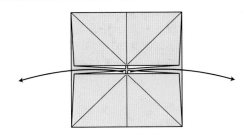

5 Pinch the inner corners of the bottom portion from the centre and pull them outwards.

2 Fold the four corners to the centre, then unfold. Turn the piece over.

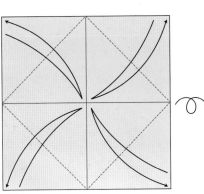

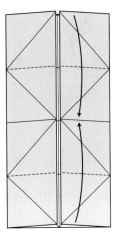

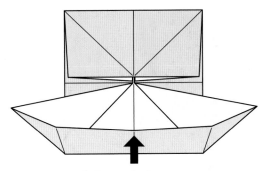

6 Flatten the bottom. Repeat step 5 on the top portion.

4 Fold the top and bottom edges to meet at the centre crease.

These snowflake-like charms start with a boat base. See page 98.

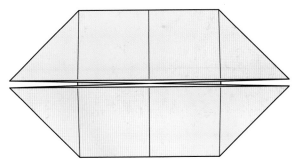

7 The finished boat base.

FLOWER BASE

1 Begin with a preliminary base (see pages 20–21).

2 Placing the base with open corners down, fold the right-hand side of the top layer to align with the centre line, then unfold.

3 Loosen an opening in the top right, and fold to the left, forming a diamond shape.

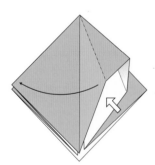

4 Flatten the diamond and press down firmly.

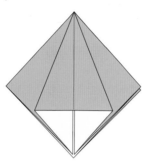

5 Repeat steps 2, 3 and 4 on the remaining three faces to make the finished flower base.

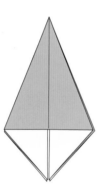

BIRD BASE

1 Begin with a preliminary base (see pages 20–21).

2 Placing the base with open corners down, fold the right and left lower edges of the top flaps to meet at the centre.

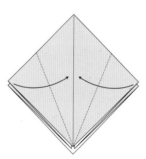

3 Fold the top triangle down and unfold, then also unfold the folds made in step 2.

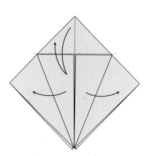

4 Lift the bottom point of the top layer and swing it upwards, keeping the top triangle closed.

keep this triangle part closed

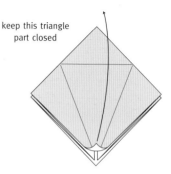

5 Push the left and right corners towards each other, so that both edges meet at the centre. Press flat.

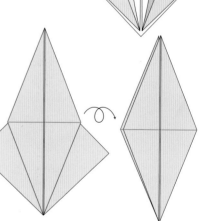

6 Turn the piece over. Repeat steps 2, 3, 4 and 5 on the other side.

Building blocks

This section provides step-by-step folding instructions for making pieces that are the building blocks for all the modular and beaded origami jewellery designs featured in this book.

These modular pieces are surprisingly simple to fold.

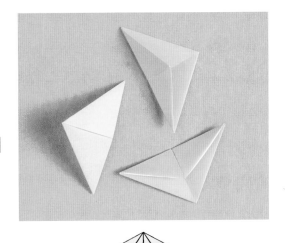

MODULAR PIECES A, B AND C

Modular piece A has corners with several layers of paper, making them thicker and more durable. Modular piece B has thinner corners that are easier to insert into other pieces. Modular piece C has one thick corner and one thin corner. Modular pieces B and C are easier to insert into other pieces.

The choice of modular pieces for a project depends on where they will be used, and the thickness of the paper. When working with very thin paper, it may be better to make modular piece A even where the instructions are for modular piece B or C.

6 Tuck the two folded-down corners underneath the bottom layer.

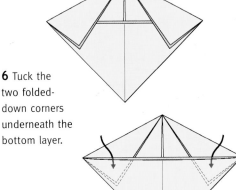

7 Fold the triangular flaps down.

8 This is the finished modular piece A.

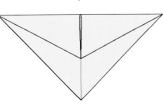

PIECE A

1 Fold in half lengthways.

3 Fold the two bottom corners inwards so that the bottom edges meet along the centre.

2 Fold in half widthways and unfold.

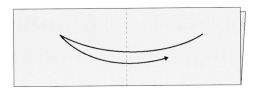

4 Turn the piece over.

5 Fold the top outer corners down.

PIECE B

1 Follow steps 1 to 4 for piece A. Then cut off the top two corners.

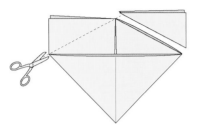

2 Fold the triangular flaps down.

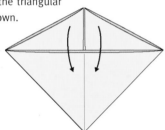

3 This is the finished modular piece B.

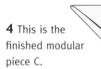

PIECE C

1 Follow steps 1 to 4 for piece A. Then cut off the top left corner. Fold the right top corner down.

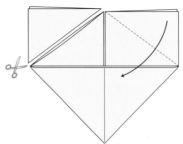

2 Tuck the right corner underneath the bottom layer.

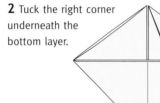

3 Fold the triangular flaps down.

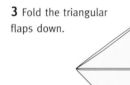

4 This is the finished modular piece C.

The folds are so simple that most types of paper work well for modular pieces.

ARMS AND POCKETS

The terms "arm" and "pocket" are used for the sections of the modules that fit together. They are shown as left and right arms and pockets.

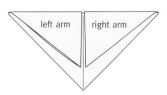
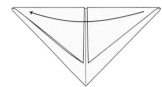
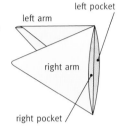

ASSEMBLING MODULAR PIECES

Before assembling modular pieces, it is helpful to put them together in the way they should be connected. This widens the pockets, making it easier to apply glue inside and insert the arms. Also, you will be less likely to make a mistake about which piece to insert, and in which order.

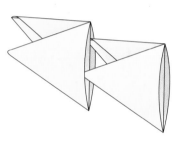

POCKET OPENER PIECES

To widen the pockets of the end piece, use two or three modular pieces A made with any paper. These will be useful "tools" to open the pockets in pieces for any modular project.

This is a great example of how simple pieces, when added together, can be transformed into an elaborate creation. This brooch is made of sixty-four modular pieces cleverly combined – see page 66.

FLOWER BEADS A AND B

1 Begin with a blintz base (see page 21) made from washi paper. Unfold the paper.

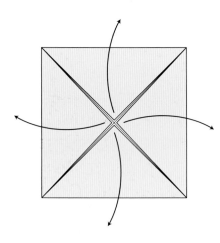

2 Using a glue stick, apply glue all over the inside, and refold the blintz base. Let the glue dry completely before proceeding to the next step.

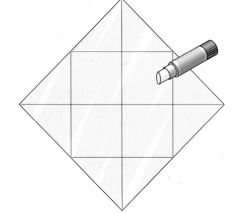

3 Bring all four corners to the centre.

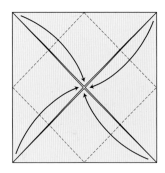

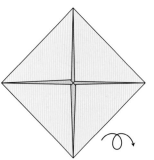

4 Turn the piece over.

5 Bring all four corners to the centre.

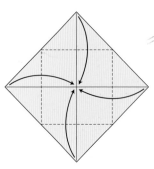

Flower earrings, page 58

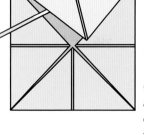

6 Lift all four triangular flaps and apply a small amount of epoxy glue underneath. Turn the piece over.

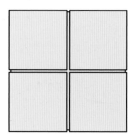

NOTE: Origami paper is not suitable for flower beads as it will tear too easily. Use washi paper instead.

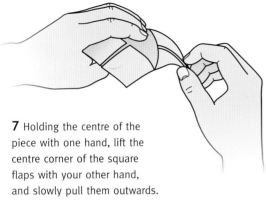

7 Holding the centre of the piece with one hand, lift the centre corner of the square flaps with your other hand, and slowly pull them outwards.

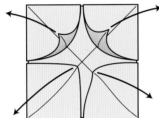

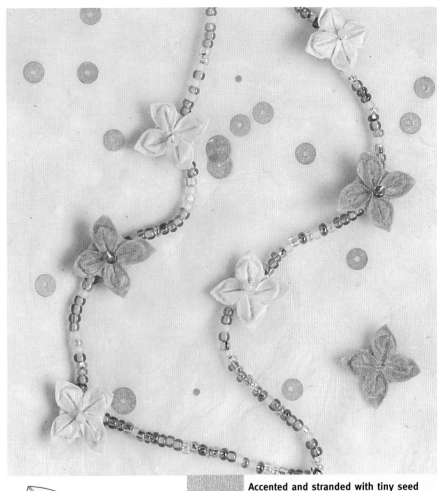

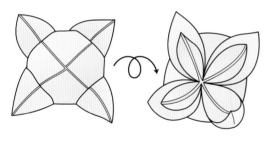

8 Turn the piece over. This is flower bead A.

Accented and stranded with tiny seed beads, these flower beads make an adorable necklace. See page 60.

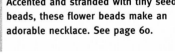

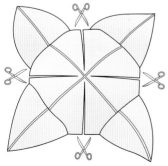

9 With the back of the piece facing up, slit between the petals towards the centre, but do not cut all the way to the centre.

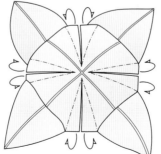

10 Mountain-fold the slits and tuck them in between layers behind petals.

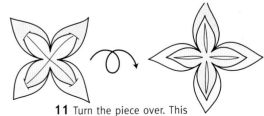

11 Turn the piece over. This is flower bead B.

CHUNKY BEAD

1 Begin with a balloon base (see page 22).

2 Fold the two bottom corners of the top layer to meet at the top corner point.

3 Fold both right and left corners of the top layer to meet at the centre.

4 Fold the top triangle flaps in half.

5 Fold the triangles down, then unfold them.

6 Loosen both pockets. Insert the triangles in the pockets.

7 Turn the piece over.

8 Repeat steps 2 to 6 on the other side.

9 Using the tip of a toothpick, apply a small amount of epoxy glue into and behind the pockets.

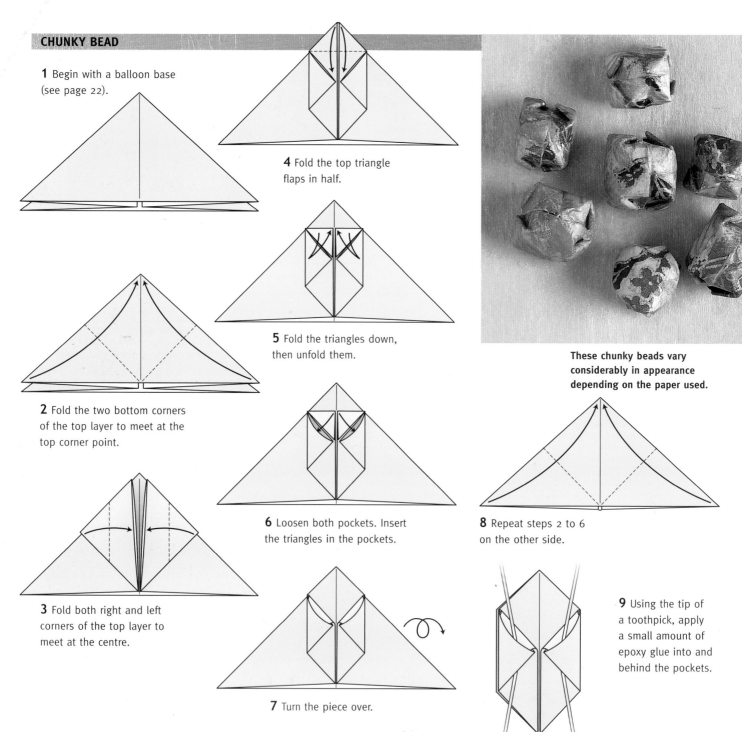

These chunky beads vary considerably in appearance depending on the paper used.

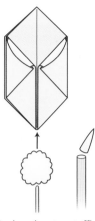

10 Push polyester stuffing into the piece from the small hole at the bottom. Use a blunt toothpick to push it in. (A sharp or pointed stuffing toothpick will penetrate the stuffing, rather than push it into place.)

11 The piece is ready to be coated and used as an origami bead.

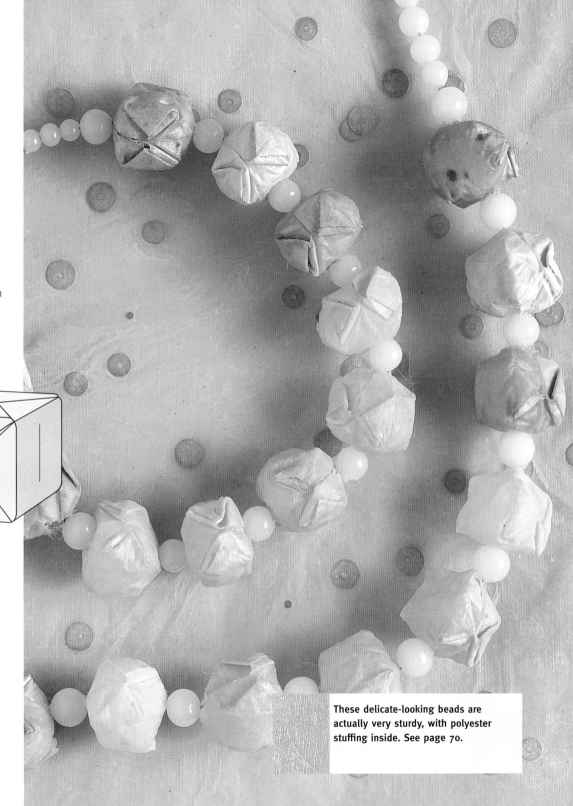

NOTE: You can stop at step 9, and use the flat piece as a bead, too. It can be used showing the faces with or without triangle pockets.

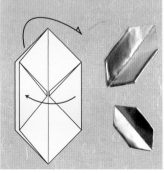

These delicate-looking beads are actually very sturdy, with polyester stuffing inside. See page 70.

PINECONE BEAD

1 Begin with a flower base (see page 24).

2 Unfold the paper completely. Fold the four corners into the middle, then refold the base.

the paper when completely flattened out

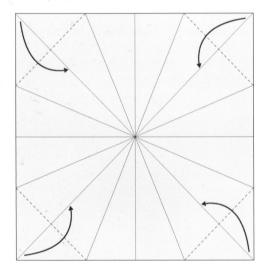

3 This is how the piece should look after refolding the base.

4 Fold the bottom corners of the top layer up to align with the centre line, then unfold.

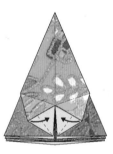

5 Loosen an opening and push the two corners inside, then flatten them.

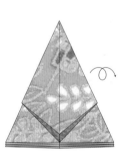

6 Turn over, then repeat steps 4 and 5 on the other side.

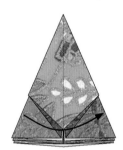

7 Fold one flap to the side, then repeat steps 4 and 5 on that side.

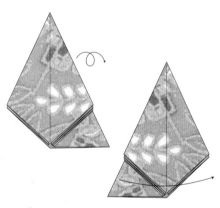

8 Turn over, fold one flap on the side, then repeat steps 4 and 5 on that side.

9 This is how the piece should look at the end of step 8.

10 Using the tip of a toothpick, apply a small amount of epoxy glue between the flaps.

11 Press both sides of each flap together with your fingers and form the piece into a cone shape. The pinecone bead is ready for coating and using as an origami bead.

NOTE: When coating the bead, make sure the flaps do not stick to each other.

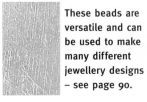

These beads are versatile and can be used to make many different jewellery designs – see page 90.

Finishing jewellery

Some people worry about the idea of wearing paper: "It's so delicate, I'll destroy it within a day!" or "What if it rains?" The techniques explained in this section show how to turn your origami creations into lovely pieces to wear without worry. Durability has a lot to do with the choice of paper, so do read the information on choosing paper. To optimize the performance of a coating, follow the folding and gluing, and padding stages. Of course, origami is not as durable as metal, but if you use the right materials and coat the pieces properly, the jewellery is surprisingly durable, and you can wear it even on rainy days!

Folding and gluing

The finishing steps for each project show how and where to apply glue during folding. Remember to smooth the glued surface and let the glue dry completely before making the next fold.

Using polyester stuffing

Padding makes pieces that have large empty spaces between layers more sturdy and prevents them from being squashed – for example, padding chunky beads makes them more durable. Padding is also an effective way to give some pieces – such as the rabbit, kimono and frog brooches – a fluffy appearance, instead of a flat look. Some pieces have a small hole through which stuffing can be pushed using a blunt toothpick. Remember that a pointed toothpick will cut through the stuffing, making it difficult to push it into the piece).

For jewellery made from multiple pieces, such as this wreath brooch (see page 102), it is essential to apply glue to maintain strength.

POLYESTER STUFFING
This filling gives durability and a more three-dimensional look.

A toothpick will come in handy to glue hard-to-reach areas and between layers.

CAUTION!

Foil and opalescent paper are not suitable for coating. Some paper bleeds when wet, so coat a scrap piece of paper to check. First, be sure to read the manufacturer's directions and cautions before applying coating.

Final gluing

Most origami models do not need glue to maintain their shape. Even so, applying a little glue here and there makes some pieces sturdier, which means you do not have to worry about areas unfolding when the jewellery is worn. For this, use waterproof epoxy glue that dries like clear rubber. A round toothpick is a great tool for applying glue between layers and in hard-to-reach areas. Always follow the manufacturer's directions and cautions.

PADDING

Some pieces have a small hole through which polyester stuffing can be pushed using a blunt toothpick – a pointed toothpick will cut through the stuffing, making it difficult to push it into the piece.

DRYING

While drying the coated pieces, make sure that the pieces and the flaps are not touching, or they will stick together and cannot be separated when dry. After the first coating, the piece might slightly lose its shape. Reshape it before the second coating.

Smooth the glued surface with fingers or a bone folder.

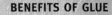

BENEFITS OF GLUE

The crane on the left was folded and coated, but the one on the right had its wing layers glued shut before coating. Comparing the two pieces from underneath shows that the thin layer of glue makes the paper slightly stiff and gives the crane on the right a crisp appearance.

Coating

There is more than one way to coat origami jewellery. I recommend using polyurethane, which is also used as a découpage medium. Polyurethane will soak through the paper to coat the entire piece, not just the surface. It is water based and therefore easy to handle, but, when dry, it is water resistant. Polyurethane makes the paper stiff but maintains flexibility, so the piece will not crack. It is available in mat, satin, semi-gloss, gloss and high-gloss finishes. Use satin or matt finish to keep the warm look of paper, unless you prefer a shinier finish. Even the satin and matt finishes make the paper slightly shinier and darker in colour.

Foil and opalescent paper are not suitable for coating. Some paper bleeds when wet, so coat a scrap piece of paper to check if it bleeds. First, be sure to read the manufacturer's directions and cautions before applying coating. All the glued areas should be completely dry before coating. If you feel the

Coating with polyurethane

From a small amount of polyurethane in a container, apply a thin layer with a small paintbrush to all surfaces and small spaces between layers. Let dry completely. Repeat two or three times.

piece needs more coats, coat the areas where that will not show, such as behind the wings and between the layers of the crane's beaks.

Do not dip the piece in the coating material, or pour the coating material over the piece. If the piece gets too wet, it will start to unfold. Generous coating gives good durability but less beauty.

To dry the coated pieces, lay them, facing up, on wax paper or another non-stick surface. Make sure that the pieces or flaps are not touching during drying or they will stick together and cannot be separated when dry.

Other coating methods

You may like to experiment with any of these coating methods:
+ Clear nail polish can be used to coat a small piece, but it tends to make the piece shiny, it protects only the surface of the paper, and it may crack where it bends.

Toothpicks stuck into an eraser make an innovative drying rack for smaller pieces.

+ Acrylic spray is simple and quick for coating, but it does not make the finished piece as durable as polyurethane.
+ Heavy, pour-on or dip-in varnish can make a piece very durable and waterproof; however, this makes the piece look more like shiny plastic or clay.
+ Oil-based varnishes will give a yellow-tinted finish.

Paper bleeding

Some origami papers bleed. If this happens, colours may run or smear during coating, and, even when coated, if exposed to excess water. Good-quality yuzen washi paper does not bleed (or it bleeds so little that it does not matter). Mujizome (solid-colour) washi paper tends to bleed, but the ink is soaked through the paper, so you will not lose the colour.

Test a scrap piece of paper for bleeding to be sure. To avoid unwanted colour mixing, change or wash the brush when applying coating to different coloured papers. Using a tapping motion with the brush minimizes smearing. Applying additional layers of coating should minimize further bleeding, but it might not completely prevent it.

To avoid wasting your best paper, first coat a scrap piece to check if the paper bleeds when wet.

Fixing findings

Attaching jewellery findings (or fittings) is the final stage. All the techniques required for completing the projects in the book are explained here.

Samurai helmet earrings, page 118

FIXING A CRIMP BEAD

Crimp beads are made of soft metal and are used to hold other beads in place or connect findings to the beading wire.

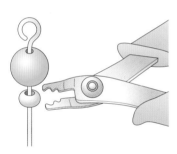

1 Thread the crimp bead on the pin or wire.

2 Pinch and flatten the crimp bead firmly using crimping pliers.

OPENING AND CLOSING A JUMP RING

1 Using two pairs of round-nose pliers, pry the jump ring open by pushing one end away from you, and, at the same time, pulling the other end towards you.

2 Do the reverse to close.

ATTACHING A CLASP TO THREAD

This technique is also used for an end bar and split ring.

1 Tie the thread to the clasp.

2 Apply clear nail polish to the knot for an extra safeguard against it coming undone.

3 Thread a few beads so that the loose end of the thread is inside the beads.

4 Then trim the end of the thread. Use this technique at the other end of the thread to attach a split ring.

Paper crane earrings, page 111

ATTACHING A CLASP TO BEADING WIRE

This technique is also used for an end bar and split ring.

1 Thread a crimp bead on the wire, then loop the wire through the clasp and back through the bead.

2 Slide the crimp bead down the wire, to about 2.5 mm (1/8 in.) from the clasp.

3 Use crimping pliers to flatten the bead.

4 Thread a few beads so that the loose end of the wire is inside them. Then trim the end of the wire. Do the same on the other end of the wire to attach a split ring.

ATTACHING A CLASP TO CORD

This technique is also used for an end bar and split ring.

To make the leaf shown here, turn to page 82.

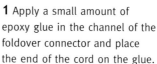

1 Apply a small amount of epoxy glue in the channel of the foldover connector and place the end of the cord on the glue.

2 Use crimping pliers to fold one flap over the cord, and crimp it tight. Fold the other side over the top of the first flap and crimp it tight and flat.

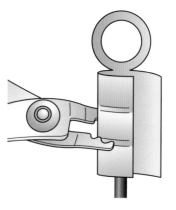

3 Add the jump ring and clasp. Do the same on the other end of the cord to attach the connector and split ring.

TER 1 Finishing jewellery

FORMING A LOOP IN A PIN

1 Cut the pin, leaving 1 cm (3/8 in.) exposed.

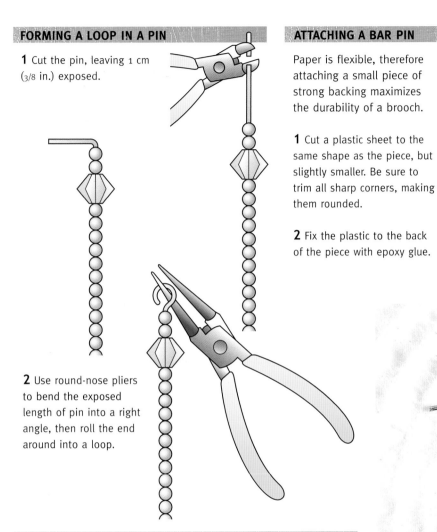

2 Use round-nose pliers to bend the exposed length of pin into a right angle, then roll the end around into a loop.

ATTACHING A BAR PIN

Paper is flexible, therefore attaching a small piece of strong backing maximizes the durability of a brooch.

1 Cut a plastic sheet to the same shape as the piece, but slightly smaller. Be sure to trim all sharp corners, making them rounded.

2 Fix the plastic to the back of the piece with epoxy glue.

3 Glue a bar pin on the plastic. Position the pin on the upper portion of the piece, otherwise the brooch will tilt down when worn.

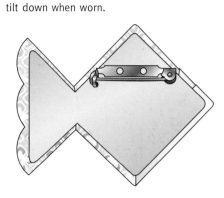

ATTACHING FISH-HOOK EARRING FINDINGS

1 Use round-nose pliers to open the loop of the finding.

2 Attach the piece, then close the loop. Make sure the piece is facing the front.

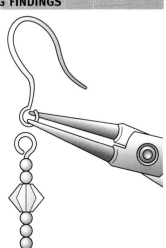

Fish-hook earring attachments are an easy way to transform your beautiful origami creations into jewellery.

SPRING
Pages 42–61

After the grey days of a long, cold winter, treat yourself with dazzling garden flowers that will never fade; display spring spirit wearing a cute rabbit or chick brooch; and create beautiful fluttering butterflies that help us fully enjoy this wonderful time of year.

AUTUMN
Pages 82–93

Autumn is the season of colour. Bright summer colours of red, yellow and green turn into the rich, saturated tones of autumn leaves. The subtler and warmer hues – such as pumpkin orange, moss green and earthy brown – inspire the artist in all of us. Experiment with combinations of colours to create your own autumnal shades.

JAPANESE
Pages 108–123

Origami designs can transcend seasons. Everyday objects from traditional Japanese life and folklore can be rendered in paper and worn with stunning effect. This traditional theme is echoed by using washi paper, so even if you've never been to Japan, you can always carry the Oriental spirit with you.

SUMMER
Pages 62–81

Close your eyes: what do you remember from summers in your childhood, or even last summer? Warm sunshine, combing for seashells on the beach with sand between your toes, colourful candyfloss at a carnival? Everything relaxes in summer, so be carefree and embrace your memories with these gorgeous origami jewellery projects.

WINTER
Pages 94–107

Winter is cold and brisk, so we search for things to keep us feeling warm. The festive holidays we celebrate, the bright stars in the crisp night sky, beautiful snowflakes on a wintry day, and the art of paper-folding – all contribute to making us feel good in this magical season.

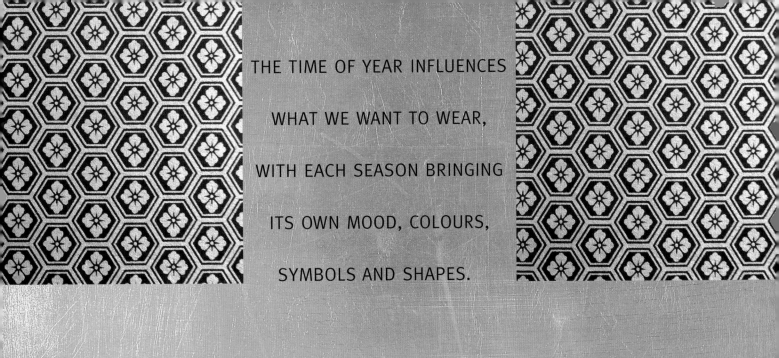

THE TIME OF YEAR INFLUENCES

WHAT WE WANT TO WEAR,

WITH EACH SEASON BRINGING

ITS OWN MOOD, COLOURS,

SYMBOLS AND SHAPES.

DIRECTORY OF DESIGNS

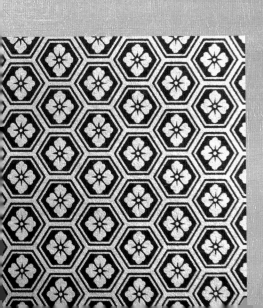

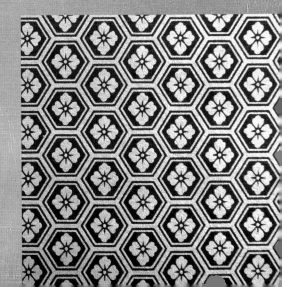

THE FOLLOWING PROJECTS

WILL KEEP YOU FOLDING

AND ACCESSORIZING ALL

THROUGH THE YEAR,

AND BEYOND...

Rose brooch, barrette and earrings

Skill level: ❖

Red, pink, yellow or white – everyone has a favourite colour for roses, so choose yours for these gorgeous blooms. Made from several identically folded flowers of different sizes, these roses are quite simple to fold, yet they look very elaborate.

FOLDING INSTRUCTIONS

For the brooch, you will need to make five of Flower Bead A (see page 28), one each in five different sizes. For the barrette, you will need to make nine of Flower Bead A, three each in three different sizes. For the earrings, you will need to make six of Flower Bead A, two each in three different sizes.

YOU WILL NEED

Brooch
+ red mujizome washi paper
  10 cm (4 in.) square
  9 cm (3½ in.) square
  6.5 cm (2½ in.) square
  5 cm (2 in.) square
  4 cm (1½ in.) square
+ 1 glass bead
+ 2.5 cm (1 in.) plastic disc
+ 2.5 cm (1 in.) bar pin

Barrette
+ red mujizome washi paper
  6.5 cm (2½ in.) squares (x 3)
  5 cm (2 in.) squares (x 3)
  4 cm (1½ in.) squares (x 3)
  10 x 4 cm (4 x 1½ in.) sheet
+ green mujizome washi paper
  2.5 cm (1 in.) squares (x 2)
+ 3 glass beads
+ 7.5 x 1.25 cm (3 x ½ in.) plastic sheet
+ 7 cm (2¾ in.) French-style barrette

Earrings
+ red mujizome washi paper
  6.5 cm (2½ in.) squares (x 2)
  5 cm (2 in.) squares (x 2)
  4 cm (1½ in.) squares (x 2)
+ 2 glass beads
+ 1.25 cm (½ in.) plastic discs (x 2)
+ 8 mm (5⁄16 in.) earring posts and nuts (x 2)

+ glue stick
+ epoxy glue
+ coating material and brush
+ round toothpick to apply glue
+ scissors
+ sewing needle
+ beading awl

Vivid variations
While solid paper gives a more realistic appearance, yuzen washi and other patterned paper is more impressionistic.

FOLDING A LEAF

1 Begin with a blintz base (see page 21). Fold in half to form a triangle.

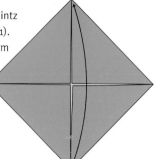

2 Fold the bottom edge up a little from one corner.

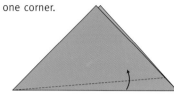

3 Unfold the bottom layer.

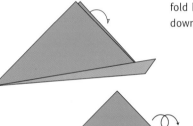

4 Flatten the centre fold by folding it down, in half.

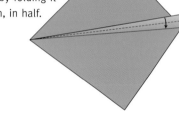

5 Turn the piece over.

6 Fold the top and bottom corners to the centre, at a slight angle.

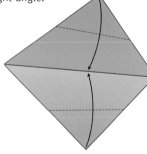

7 Fold the points of the corners to give the leaf a rounder edge.

8 Turn the piece over to show the finished side of the leaf.

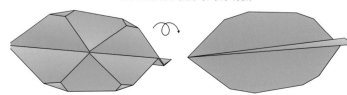

ASSEMBLING THE BROOCH

Make five of Flower Bead A, using the five different paper sizes.

1 Using epoxy glue, stack and glue the flower beads together, from smallest to largest.

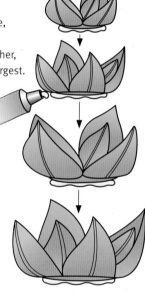

2 Coat the piece and let dry completely.

CONTINUED ON NEXT PAGE ▶

3 Insert a threaded needle from the centre back of the rose to the front. Thread a bead, then push the needle and thread back through the centre of the rose.

4 Tie the thread ends at the back to secure the bead.

5 Using epoxy glue, fix a plastic disc on the back of the rose, then glue a bar pin on the plastic.

6 Shape the completed rose petals gently with fingertips.

ASSEMBLING THE BARRETTE

Make nine of Flower Bead A, three each in three sizes, to make three roses.

1 Glue the two smallest flower beads together to make a combined piece. Do not glue the largest flower bead in place.

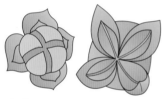

▲ **2** Coat the combined pieces and large flower beads, and let dry completely.

3 Secure a bead in the centre of the combined piece as for the brooch (steps 3 and 4).

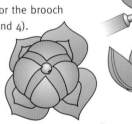

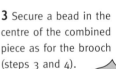

4 Glue the combined piece into the large flower bead. Make two more roses.

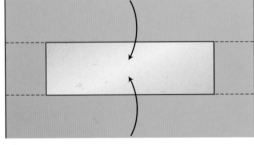

5 Make two leaves with green paper: apply glue first inside the blintz base, as done for Flower Beads. Coat the leaves and let dry completely.

6 Apply glue stick all over the inside of the red 10 x 4 cm (4 x 1 1/2 in.) paper. Centre the plastic sheet on the glued paper. Fold the top and bottom edges over to cover the plastic.

▶ **7** Fold the corners in slightly. Apply glue to the ends and fold them over the covered plastic.

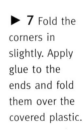

▼ **8** Turn the covered plastic over, coat it and let dry completely.

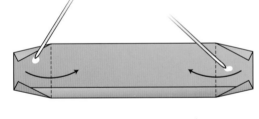

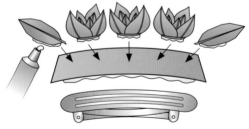

9 Using epoxy glue, glue a barrette to the wrapped plastic. Then glue two leaves and three roses on the top. To complete the barrette, shape the petals gently with fingertips.

ASSEMBLING THE EARRINGS

Make six of Flower Bead A. Follow steps 1 to 3 for the barrette.

1 Use a beading awl to pierce a hole in the centres of the large flower beads and the plastic discs.

2 Insert an earring post through the largest piece and the plastic disc. Apply epoxy glue to secure the post and plastic disc to the flower bead.

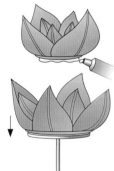

3 Glue the combined piece on the large flower bead.

4 Shape the petals with fingers. Attach an earring nut to complete the earrings.

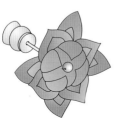

Solid paper gives a vivid impact. These cardinal-red roses will catch everyone's eye.

Butterfly brooch, hairpin, bracelet and earrings

Skill level:

brooch, hairpin ❖ ❖

bracelet, earrings ❖ ❖ ❖

The butterfly is a symbol of beauty, transformation and freedom. Butterflies have always been loved, worldwide, for their graceful appearance as they flutter freely in the air. Yuzen washi paper is recommended to represent the butterfly's beauty.

Capture and wear these fluttery butterflies. A bar pin with bail enables the brooch to also be worn as a pendant, and the bail represents the butterfly's antennae.

YOU WILL NEED

Brooch

+ 7.5 cm (3 in.) square yuzen washi paper
+ 4 cm (1½ in.) plastic disc or 4 x 2.5 cm (1½ x 1 in.) plastic sheet
+ 4 cm (1½ in.) bar pin

Hairpin

+ 5 cm (2 in.) square yuzen washi paper
+ hairpin

Bracelet

+ 4 cm (1½ in.) squares yuzen washi paper (x 3)
+ 3 Swarovski beads
+ 2.5 cm (1 in.) eye pins (x 3)
+ 15 cm (6 in.) gold-plated chain
+ 2 split rings
+ clasp

Earrings

+ 4 cm (1½ in.) squares yuzen washi paper (x 2)
+ 2 Swarovski beads
+ 4 seed beads
+ 2.5 cm (1 in.) eye pins (x 2)
+ 2 fish-hook earring findings

+ glue stick
+ epoxy glue
+ coating material and brush
+ round toothpick to apply glue
+ scissors
+ beading awl or needle
+ round-nose pliers
+ cutting pliers

FOLDING INSTRUCTIONS

For smaller pieces, omit the antennae to make folding a little easier; however, if you wish, you can add them.

FOLDING THE BUTTERFLY

1 Fold the square in half, making a centre crease, then unfold.

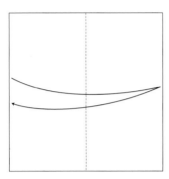

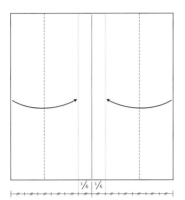

2 Fold both sides to about one-sixth away from the centre crease.

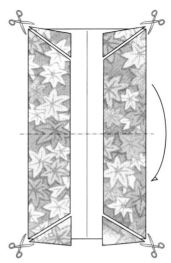

◄ 3 Trim the four corners off the folded layers. Mountain-fold in half lengthways.

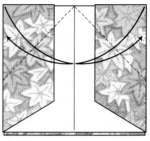

4 Fold both top corners to meet the centre crease, then unfold.

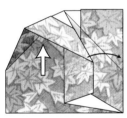
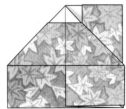

5 Loosen the left half opening and bring the left edge all the way to the right edge, forming a triangle. Flatten the triangle. Turn the piece over, and do the same on the other side.

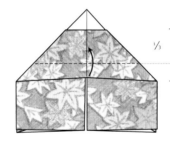

6 Fold up the bottom of the triangle by about one third.

7 Loosen both right and left openings, forming triangles. Flatten the triangles to make the butterfly's wings.

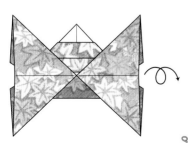

8 Turn over and rotate the piece.

9 Make four cuts from the sides of the wings, as shown. Fold following the direction of the arrows.

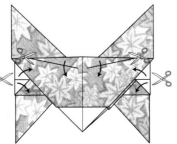

10 Fold up the butterfly's antennae. Turn the butterfly over.

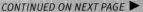

CONTINUED ON NEXT PAGE ▶

11 Mountain-fold the centre of the butterfly, and valley-fold the ends of the wings.

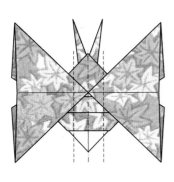

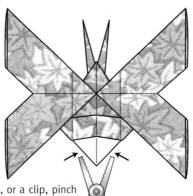

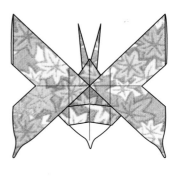

13 Pinch the two bottom points of the wings to complete the butterfly.

12 Using fingers, or a clip, pinch the bottom point of the butterfly.

ASSEMBLING THE BROOCH

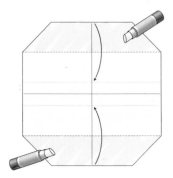

3 Cut a plastic disc or sheet for the back of the butterfly, as shown, making it slightly smaller than the butterfly. Using epoxy glue, fix the plastic to the back of the butterfly, then glue a bar pin to the plastic.

FRONT
(glue where indicated by toothpicks)

1 Fold the butterfly up to and including step 3, then unfold and apply glue stick on the folds, refold and complete.

2 Using the tip of a toothpick, apply epoxy glue between loose layers of the butterfly. Apply epoxy glue to pinched points (as in steps 12 and 13 of folding), and pinch them again, holding until glue dries. Apply epoxy glue on the back of the butterfly's antennae to make them more durable. Coat the piece and let dry completely.

BACK
(glue where indicated by toothpicks)

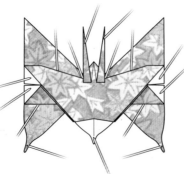

ASSEMBLING THE HAIRPIN

Follow steps 1 and 2 for the brooch. Glue the butterfly on a hairpin using epoxy glue. When using a thin hairpin, pull a thread through the butterfly and tie it around the pin, then apply epoxy glue for strength.

ASSEMBLING THE BRACELET

Make three butterflies, omitting to fold the antennae in steps 9 and 10. Follow steps 1 and 2 for the brooch.

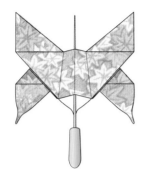

1 Holding the butterfly with the back uppermost, insert a beading awl from the bottom, through the top layer, and pierce the top of the butterfly.

2 Thread a Swarovski bead on an eye pin. Insert the pin through the pierced hole, from the top. Cut off the bottom of the eye pin, leaving about 5 mm (1/4 in.) exposed. Use the round-nose pliers to bend up the bottom of the eye pin.

glue

3 Using a toothpick, apply epoxy glue down the centre of the butterfly. With your fingers or a clip, hold the wings closed over the folded-back pin until the glue dries to secure it in place.

4 Attach a split ring and clasp to the chain. Use round-nose pliers to connect the loops of the eye pins on the butterflies to the chain, placing one in the middle, and two others at equal distances away from it.

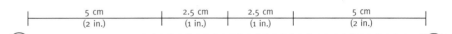

5 cm (2 in.)	2.5 cm (1 in.)	2.5 cm (1 in.)	5 cm (2 in.)

ASSEMBLING THE EARRINGS

Make two butterflies. As for the bracelet, omit making antennae. Follow steps 1 to 3 for the bracelet, threading a seed bead, a Swarovski bead and then a second seed bead on the eye pin in place of the single Swarovski bead.

1 Attach earring findings to the tops of the eye pins to complete the earrings.

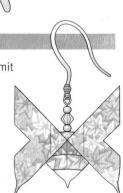

By simply connecting three tiny butterflies on a chain, you can create a matching bracelet.

Flower bouquet brooch

Skill level: ❖

Create a beautiful bouquet of flowers using simple folds. Each flower is made with six modular pieces, accented with beads in the centre. The leaves emphasize the brightness of the flowers. Using one colour for each bouquet gives impact, and different shades and paper textures impart depth.

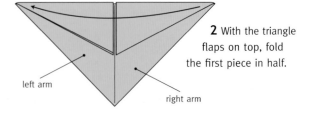

YOU WILL NEED

- ✦ 3 x 5 cm (1¼ x 2 in.) orange mujizome washi paper (x 30)
- ✦ green mujizome washi paper
  5 cm (2 in.) square
  6.5 cm (2½ in.) square
- ✦ 15 white seed beads
- ✦ orange ribbon
- ✦ beading thread
- ✦ 10 cm (4 in.) length 22-gage floral wire (x 7)
- ✦ 4 cm (1½ in.) plastic disc or 4 cm (1½ in.) square plastic sheet
- ✦ 3 cm (1¼ in.) bar pin
- ✦ epoxy glue
- ✦ coating material and brush
- ✦ toothpick to apply glue
- ✦ scissors
- ✦ cutting pliers
- ✦ round-nose pliers

FOLDING INSTRUCTIONS

Make 30 of Modular Piece C, six for each flower (see page 26). If using thin paper, you can make Piece A instead of Piece C, to give more durability. For leaves, make one each in two different sizes, following the folding instructions for the leaves on the Rose Barrette (see page 43).

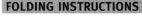

ASSEMBLING THE FLOWERS

1 You will need six of Modular Piece C for each flower.

2 With the triangle flaps on top, fold the first piece in half.

left arm

right arm

> Vary these flower bouquets any way you like. Alternate colour, shade and texture of paper, and accent with different beads and bows to match your outfit.

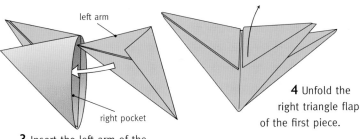

left arm

right pocket

3 Insert the left arm of the second piece into right pocket of the first piece.

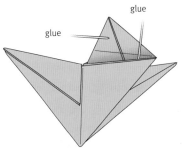

4 Unfold the right triangle flap of the first piece.

glue

glue

glue

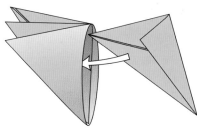

6 Repeat steps 3, 4 and 5 with the remaining four pieces. After inserting the left arm of the sixth piece into the right pocket of the fifth piece, insert the left arm of the first piece into the right pocket of the sixth piece.

5 Using the tip of a toothpick, apply small amounts of epoxy glue inside the pocket and on the triangle flap. Fold the triangle flap back.

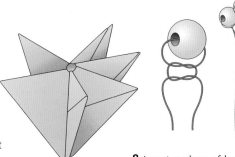

7 The first flower is completed: make four more, then coat them and let dry completely.

8 Insert a piece of beading thread through a seed bead and secure with a double knot. Prepare three for each flower.

9 Use round-nose pliers to bend the tip of a piece of floral wire. Tie three beads on the top of the wire by twisting the threads around it. Apply epoxy glue where the threads are twisted to secure them, trimming off any excess thread.

10 Insert the floral wire into the flower, from the top. Using a toothpick, apply epoxy glue at the top and bottom of the hole to secure the wire inside the flower.

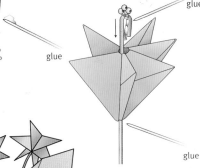

glue

glue

glue

WIRING THE LEAVES

Make two leaves, in each of two different sizes. After making a blintz base (see page 21), unfold the paper, apply glue to the inside with a glue stick, then refold. Attach wires to the leaves when folding: apply epoxy glue down the leaf centre, then place a floral wire on top. Glue down the folds made in steps 6 and 7 of folding.

glue

glue

ASSEMBLING THE BOUQUET

1 Arrange five flowers and two leaves together. Tie the wires with beading thread. Apply epoxy glue on the threads. Use cutting pliers to trim excess wires.

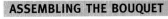

glue

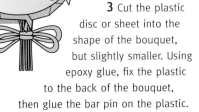

2 Tie a bow to conceal the wires.

3 Cut the plastic disc or sheet into the shape of the bouquet, but slightly smaller. Using epoxy glue, fix the plastic to the back of the bouquet, then glue the bar pin on the plastic.

Rabbit brooch

Skill level: ❖ ❖

For texture, this adorable rabbit is made with momi (hand-wrinkled) mujizome washi paper. Adding little beads for eyes gives the rabbit a cute look, though it is still lovable without them. Don't forget to add a little cotton-tail!

YOU WILL NEED

- 3½ in. (9 cm) square white washi
- 1 x ⅜ in. (2.5 x 1 cm) pink mulberry paper (x 2)
- 2 red seed beads
- 3 x 2.5 cm (1¼ x 1 in.) plastic sheet
- 2.5 cm (1 in.) bar pin
- polyester stuffing
- beading or sewing thread
- 5 mm (³⁄₁₆ in.) white pom-pom
- glue stick
- epoxy glue
- coating material and brush
- toothpick to apply glue
- scissors
- sewing needle

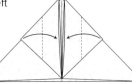
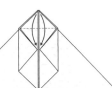
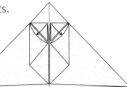
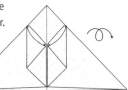

1 Begin with a balloon base (see page 22). Fold the two lower corners of the top layer to meet at the top corner.

2 Fold right and left corners of the top layer to meet at the centre.

3 Fold the top triangle flaps in half.

4 Fold the triangles down, then unfold them.

5 Loosen both pockets. Insert the triangles in the pockets.

6 Turn the piece over.

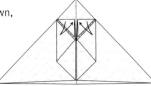
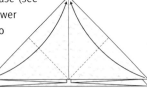

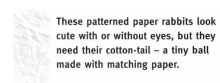

These patterned paper rabbits look cute with or without eyes, but they need their cotton-tail – a tiny ball made with matching paper.

7 Fold the right and left edges to meet at the centre.

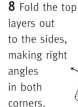

8 Fold the top layers out to the sides, making right angles in both corners.

9 Fold the bottom corners up to the centre line.

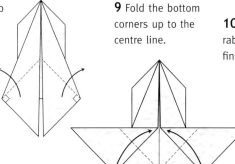

10 The completed rabbit, ready for finishing.

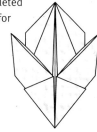

ASSEMBLING THE BROOCH

1 Use a toothpick to apply epoxy glue between the two layers of the ears and face to seal them.

glue where indicated by toothpicks

2 Cut two pieces of pink mulberry paper into shapes similar to the ears but smaller. Using glue stick, attach them to the rabbit's ears, sticking the bottom parts of the pink paper into the small openings over the rabbit's face. Use the tip of a toothpick to apply epoxy glue to seal the openings.

glue where indicated by toothpicks

3 Turn the piece over.

▼ **4** Use a toothpick to apply epoxy glue in one pocket to seal it. Unfold the other side.

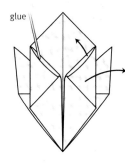

glue

5 Push stuffing inside the rabbit and fold back the pocket to close it, then apply epoxy glue to seal it. Coat the rabbit and let dry completely.

stuffing

6 Cut a piece of plastic sheet to the same shape as the bottom of the rabbit, but slightly smaller. Using epoxy glue, fix the plastic to the rabbit, then glue a bar pin to the plastic.

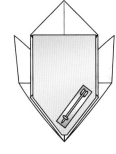

7 Turn the piece over. Sew seed beads to represent eyes on the face, threading them from the back of the face.

8 Glue the face to the body using epoxy glue.

9 Use epoxy glue to glue a pom-pom on the rabbit's behind.

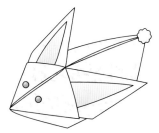

Chick in egg brooch

Skill level: ❖

Spring is a time for birth, and rebirth, and cute little chicks hatch into their new lives. Wearing this adorable brooch is a fun way to display your own "spring spirit". Both chick and egg are simple to fold.

Mujizome washi gives a fluffy, downy texture to the chick, while printer paper gives a shiny, smooth surface to the egg.

YOU WILL NEED

- 10 cm (4 in.) square yellow mujizome washi paper
- 7.5 cm (3 in.) square white paper (photocopy or printer paper)
- black seed bead
- 4 cm (1½ in.) plastic disc or 4 cm (1½ in.) square plastic
- 2.5 cm (1 in.) bar pin
- black sewing thread
- glue stick
- epoxy glue
- coating material and brush
- toothpick to apply glue
- scissors
- sewing needle

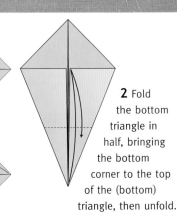

FOLDING THE CHICK

1 Begin with a blintz base (see page 21). Fold the right and left lower edges to meet at the centre.

2 Fold the bottom triangle in half, bringing the bottom corner to the top of the (bottom) triangle, then unfold.

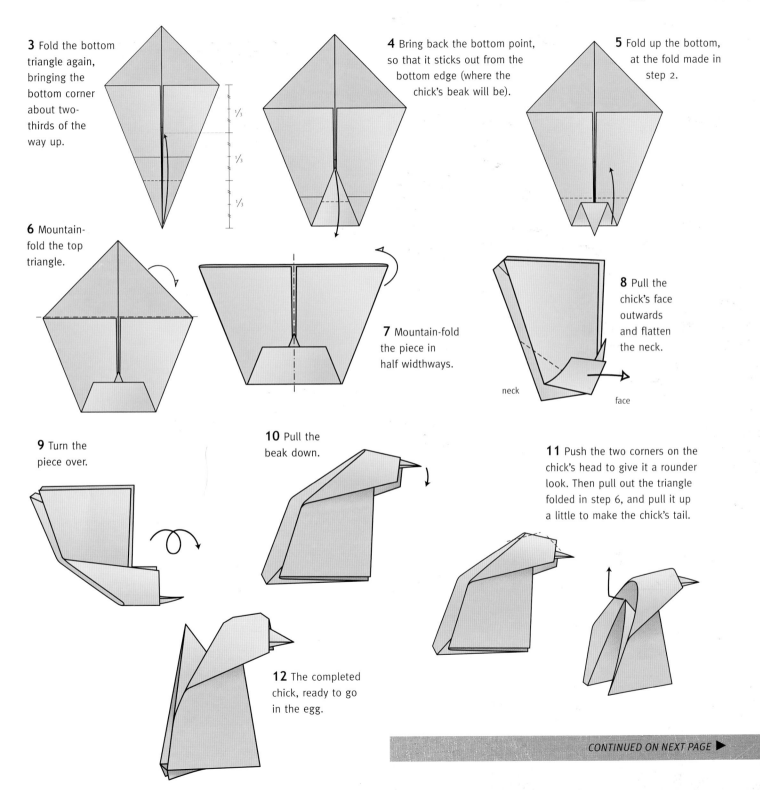

3 Fold the bottom triangle again, bringing the bottom corner about two-thirds of the way up.

$\frac{1}{3}$

$\frac{1}{3}$

$\frac{1}{3}$

4 Bring back the bottom point, so that it sticks out from the bottom edge (where the chick's beak will be).

5 Fold up the bottom, at the fold made in step 2.

6 Mountain-fold the top triangle.

7 Mountain-fold the piece in half widthways.

8 Pull the chick's face outwards and flatten the neck.

neck

face

9 Turn the piece over.

10 Pull the beak down.

11 Push the two corners on the chick's head to give it a rounder look. Then pull out the triangle folded in step 6, and pull it up a little to make the chick's tail.

12 The completed chick, ready to go in the egg.

CONTINUED ON NEXT PAGE ▶

FOLDING THE EGG

1 Begin with a blintz base (see page 21). Fold in half. Fold both right and left corners up from the centre at an angle.

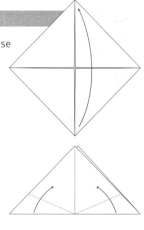

2 Mountain-fold the right, left and bottom corners to give the egg a rounder look.

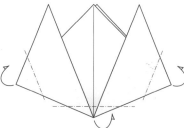

3 The finished egg will hold the chick.

ASSEMBLING THE BROOCH

1 After making a blintz base for the chick, unfold the paper completely. Using a glue stick, apply glue all over the inside of the paper, and refold it to a blintz base. Fold, then unfold the lower edges, apply glue inside, and fold them back to the center. Complete folding the chick.

2 Mountain-fold the bottom left corner so that the chick will fit in the egg. Coat the chick and let dry completely.

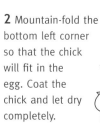

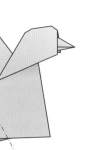

3 Sew a bead to the chick's face to represent an eye.

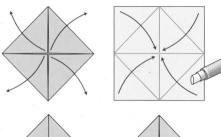

4 Using the tip of a toothpick, apply epoxy glue under the chick's face and behind the head.

glue where indicated by toothpicks

5 When folding the egg, apply glue inside the blintz base, as done for the chick in step 1. Coat the egg and let dry completely. Insert the chick in the egg.

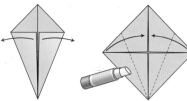

6 Apply epoxy glue on the back of the chick to secure it inside the egg.

glue

7 Cut a piece of plastic disc or sheet slightly smaller than the back of the egg. Using epoxy glue, attach it to the back of the egg, then glue a bar pin on the plastic.

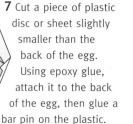

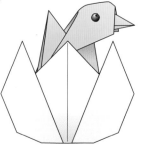

8 The completed chick peeks out at the world.

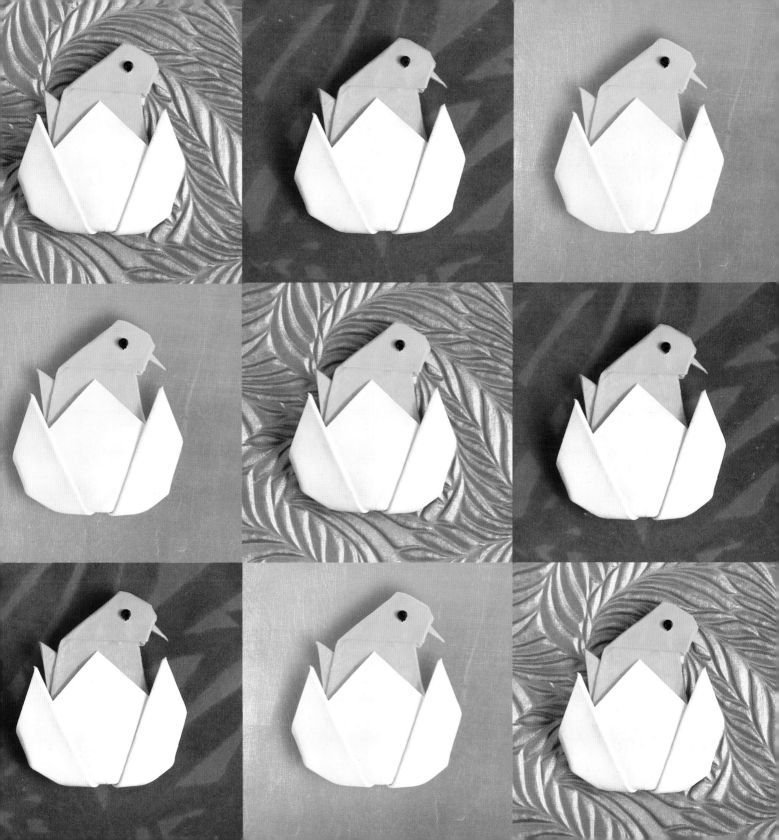

Flower choker and earrings

Skill level:

choker ❖

earrings ❖ ❖

Less is more in this stylish design, where just one set of flower beads in the centre of the choker makes a strong statement. If you wish, experiment with other types of cord in place of the twine used here, and try other knots to make the base of the choker. Matching earrings, with smaller flowers, complement the simple, elegant choker.

FOLDING INSTRUCTIONS

Follow the instructions for folding Flower Bead B (see page 28). For the choker, you need two of Flower Bead B in different sizes: one using 6.5 cm (2½ in.) square paper, and one using 4 cm (1½ in.)

square paper. For the earrings you need 12 of Flower Bead B in different sizes: eight using 4 cm (1½ in.) square paper, and four using 2.5 cm (1 in.) square paper.

YOU WILL NEED

Choker

- ✦ yuzen washi paper
  6.5 cm (2½ in.) square
  4 cm (1½ in.) square
- ✦ 2 seed beads
- ✦ 1 cm (⅜ in.) jade bead
- ✦ 3.35 m (11 feet) twine cord

Earrings

- ✦ yuzen washi paper
  4 cm (1½ in.) square (x 8)
  2.5 cm (1 in.) square (x 4)
- ✦ 12 seed beads
- ✦ 5 cm (2 in.) lengths twine cord
  (x 2)
- ✦ 2 fold-over connectors
- ✦ 2 fish-hook earring findings

- ✦ beading thread
- ✦ clear nail polish
- ✦ glue stick
- ✦ epoxy glue
- ✦ coating material and brush
- ✦ toothpick to apply glue
- ✦ scissors
- ✦ sewing needle

ASSEMBLING THE CHOKER

Make and coat the flower beads, then let dry completely.

1 Knot the twine cord to about 35.5 cm (14 in.) long (see Knotting cord, opposite). Make sure the loop at the end of the cord is slightly larger than the jade bead. Pull one end of the cord through the loop at the end of the knot. Cut the ends, leaving about 1.25 cm (½ in.).

2 Sew the ends together on to the back of the knotted cord, making sure they will not show on the front. Apply clear nail polish over the thread and cord ends, to secure them and prevent them from working loose. Sew so that the thread will not show from the front and make the loop slightly bigger than the jade bead.

3 Thread a jade bead and a seed bead together, and sew them on the other end of the knotted cord. Apply clear nail polish over the thread to prevent them working loose.

4 Insert a threaded needle through from the back of the larger flower out to the centre front. Thread it through the centre of the smaller flower (from the back), and push a seed bead on the thread. Then pull the thread back through the centres of both flowers. Apply epoxy glue between the two flowers. Tie the thread ends at the back.

5 Sew the flower in place at the centre of the knotted cord, applying epoxy glue between the flower and cord.

ASSEMBLING THE EARRINGS

Make and coat the flower beads, and let dry completely.

1 Attach a fold-over connector to the twine cord, following steps 1 and 2 for attaching a clasp to cord (page 38).

2 Insert a threaded needle from the centre back of a larger flower, pull it through to the front, thread on a seed bead, then take it to the back and tie the thread ends to secure the bead.

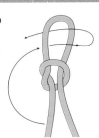

3 Sew the flower on the twin cord, right beneath the connector. Push the needle through from the back to the front of the other larger flower, through a seed bead, and then pull the thread back through the centre of the flower. Sew it to the cord. Apply epoxy glue between the flowers and cord for extra strength.

glue

4 Repeat steps 2 and 3 with the remaining two larger flowers, attaching them about 1 cm (1/2 in.) below the first pair. Then do the same with two smaller flowers, attaching them about 1 cm (1/2 in.) below the second pair of flowers. Attach earring findings (see page 39).

1.5 cm (1/2 in.)

1.5 cm (1/2 in.)

KNOTTING CORD

1 At the middle of the length of cord, make a single knot. Pull the right end through the knot.

2 Make a loop with the left end and insert it through the loop.

3 Tie the knot.

4 Make a loop with the right cord and insert it through the loop.

5 Tie the knot.

6 Repeat steps 2 to 5 until all the cord is knotted or the required length is reached.

Simple yet intricate, yuzen washi paper flower beads make a bold and elegant springtime choker.

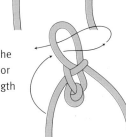

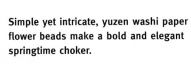

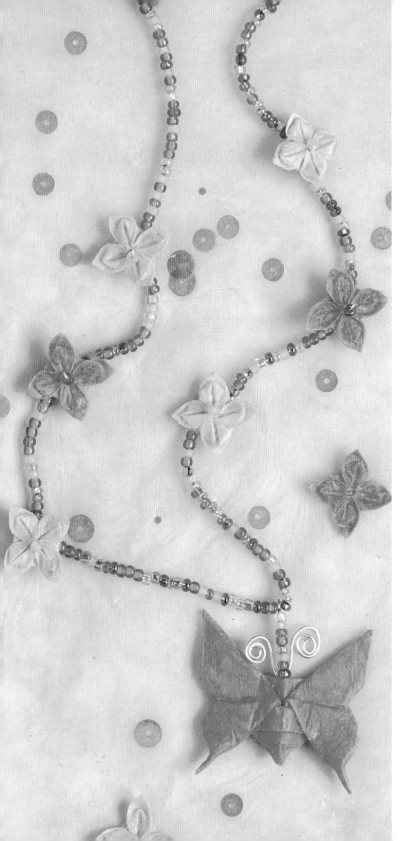

Flower beads and butterfly necklace

Skill level: ❖ ❖ ❖

This delicate design is achieved by using a few tiny origami flower beads, stranded with seed beads. The butterfly charm adds a focal point to this pretty piece.

YOU WILL NEED

+ dark pink mujizome washi paper
  4 cm (1½ in.) square (x 2)
  5 cm (2 in.) square
  2 x 1 cm (¾ x ⅜ in.) sheet
+ light pink mujizome washi paper
  4 cm (1½ in.) square (x 4)
+ 40.5 cm (16 in.) strand seed beads
+ 4 cm (1½ in.) eye pin
+ beading thread
+ 7.5 cm (3 in.) length 22-gauge silver wire
+ split ring

+ clasp
+ glue stick
+ epoxy glue
+ coating material and brush
+ toothpick to apply glue
+ scissors
+ round-nose pliers
+ cutting pliers
+ beading needle
+ clear nail polish

With a pink butterfly skimming over flower beads, this adorable necklace evokes light and airy spring days.

FOLDING INSTRUCTIONS

Make six of Flower Bead B (see page 28) in different colours, using with 4 cm (1½ in.) square paper: two in darker pink paper, and four in light pink paper. You also need one butterfly (see page 47), made using 5 cm (2 in.) square darker pink paper; omit the butterfly's antennae in steps 9 and 10.

ASSEMBLING THE NECKLACE

Follow steps 1 and 2 for Assembling the Butterfly Brooch (see page 48). Coat the flower beads. Let both butterflies and flower beads dry completely before assembling the necklace.

1 Using round-nose pliers, bend the wire in half and curl both ends, as shown. This forms the butterfly's antennae.

2 Thread eight seed beads on an eye pin. Cut the bottom of the eye pin, leaving about 1.25 cm (1/2 in.) exposed. Use round-nose pliers to bend the bottom of the eye pin in half.

1.25 cm (1/2 in.)

3 Using epoxy glue, attach the bottom of the antennae and the eye pin on the centre of the butterfly.

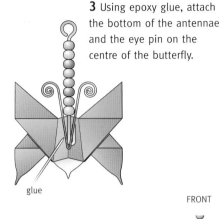

glue

4 Using epoxy glue, attach a 2 x 1 cm (3/4 x 3/8 in.) piece of paper on the back of the butterfly to cover the wires, and coat the paper.

5 Tie the beading thread to a clasp. Apply clear nail polish to the thread ends for an extra strength. Thread seed beads on the thread, to a length of 10 cm (4 in.).

FRONT

6 Push the needle on the end of the length of beads through from the centre back of the light pink flower bead to the front. Thread a seed bead, then pull the thread back through the centre of the flower to the back. Tie a knot on the back to secure the bead.

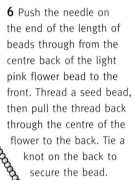

BACK

7 Thread seed beads for 2.5 cm (1 in.) and repeat the last step, using a dark pink flower bead. Thread seed beads for 2.5 cm (1 in.), then add a light pink flower bead.

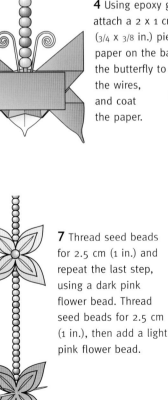

10 cm (4 in.)

2.5 cm (1 in.) 2.5 cm (1 in.) 2.5 cm (1 in.)

4 cm (1½ in.)

8 Thread seed beads for a further 4 cm (1½ in.). Then thread the loop of the eye pin attached to the butterfly on the beads. Thread seed beads for 4 cm (1½ in.). Repeat step 6, with a light pink flower bead, and step 7, with the remaining dark, and light, pink flower beads. Thread seed beads for a final 10 cm (4 in.).

9 To complete the necklace, tie the end of the thread to a split ring. Apply clear nail polish to the tied ends.

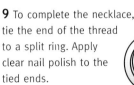

Fish brooch and earrings

Skill level:

brooch ❖

earrings ❖ ❖

One of my vivid childhood memories is proudly bringing home the goldfish I won at a summer festival. I never got bored watching them swim in their bowl. There is no need to limit the colour of goldfish, so indulge your whimsical side.

YOU WILL NEED

Brooch

+ 7.5 cm (3 in.) square yuzen washi paper
+ 7.5 cm (3 in.) square solid-colour washi paper
+ about 2.5 x 4 cm (1 x 1½ in.) plastic sheet
+ 3 cm (1¼ in.) bar pin
+ polyester stuffing

+ glue stick
+ epoxy glue
+ coating material and brush
+ round toothpick to apply glue
+ scissors
+ beading awl or needle
+ round-nose pliers
+ cutting pliers

Earrings

+ 4 cm (1½ in.) squares yuzen washi paper (x 2)
+ 4 cm (1½ in.) squares solid-colour washi paper (x 2)
+ 14 clear seed beads
+ 14 blue seed beads
+ 2 clear Swarovski beads
+ 4 cm (1.5 in.) eye pins (x 2)
+ 2 fish-hook earring findings

PREPARATION

Before starting, glue the yuzen washi and solid-colour papers back to back, using a glue stick. Let the glue dry completely before folding. For clean edges, use sheets of paper slightly larger than recommended, then trim them to the size when glued together.

FOLDING THE FISH

1 Fold in half diagonally to make a triangle.

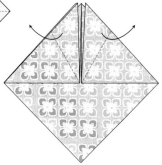

2 Fold the two corners of the long side down to meet at the bottom corner.

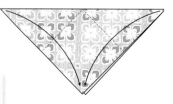

3 Fold the bottom corners of the top layer up to meet at the top corner.

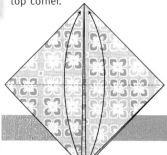

4 Fold the corners of the top layer out to extend slightly a little beyond the sides.

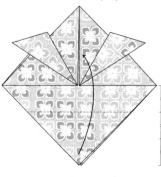

5 Fold the top layer of the bottom triangle about two-thirds of the way up.

CONTINUED ON NEXT PAGE ▶

Wavy strands of
clear bead bubbles
rise above the cheerfully
swimming fish.

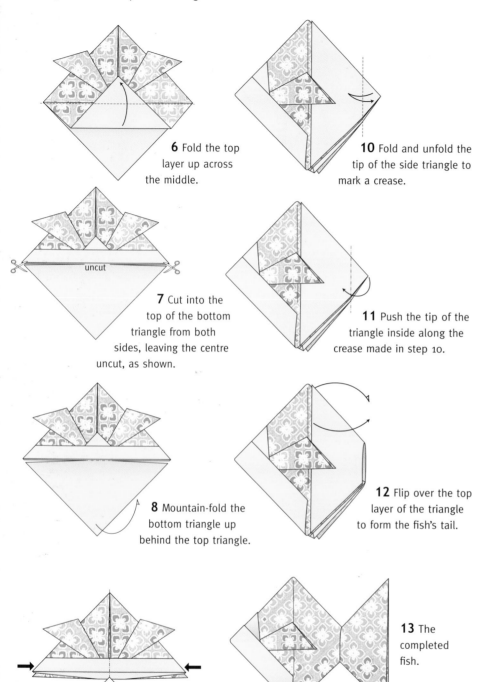

6 Fold the top layer up across the middle.

7 Cut into the top of the bottom triangle from both sides, leaving the centre uncut, as shown.

uncut

8 Mountain-fold the bottom triangle up behind the top triangle.

9 Open up the piece from the bottom, push all the way from both sides and then flatten it.

10 Fold and unfold the tip of the side triangle to mark a crease.

11 Push the tip of the triangle inside along the crease made in step 10.

12 Flip over the top layer of the triangle to form the fish's tail.

13 The completed fish.

ASSEMBLING THE BROOCH

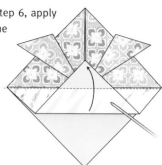

1 After folding step 6, apply epoxy glue on the top layer of the bottom portion. Then complete the folding.

2 Apply epoxy glue to the inside layers of the tail, leave to dry, and then trim the end of the tail as shown.

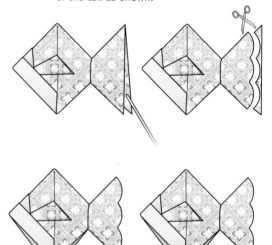

stuffing

3 Push stuffing into the body of fish and seal the opening ends with epoxy glue. Coat the piece and let it dry completely. Cut a piece of plastic sheet to the same shape as the fish, but slightly smaller. Glue it on the back of the fish, then glue a bar pin on the plastic using epoxy glue.

ASSEMBLING THE EARRINGS

1 Make two pieces and follow steps 1 and 2 for the brooch. Coat the pieces and let them dry completely. Pierce the tops of the fish with a beading awl from inside.

2 Insert an eye pin from the bottom. Apply epoxy glue to the loop of the eye pin before pulling the pin up. Leave the glue to dry inside the fish.

3 Seal the open ends of the fish with epoxy glue.

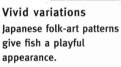

Vivid variations
Japanese folk-art patterns give fish a playful appearance.

4 Thread 12 seed beads on the pin, alternating six blue and six clear, starting with a clear one. Then slide on a Swarovski bead, followed by one more blue seed bead and one more clear. Cut the pin, leaving 1 cm (3/8 in.) exposed. Use round-nose pliers to bend the exposed portion of the eye pin into a right angle, then roll it into a loop.

5 Gently bend the bead-threaded eye pin into a wavy shape. Attach earring findings to complete the earrings.

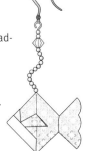

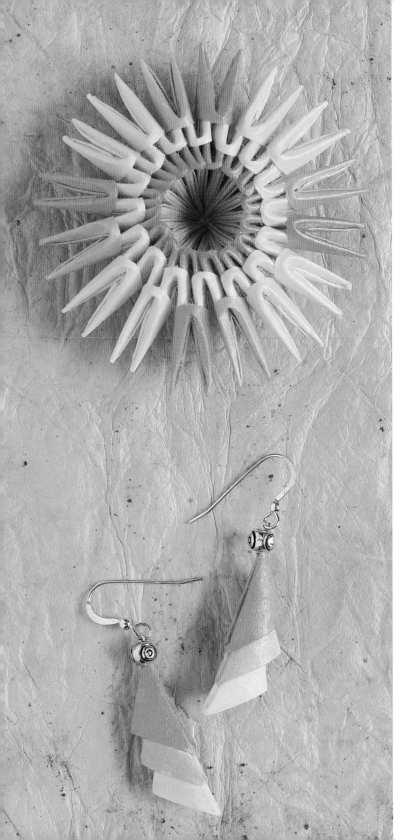

Sunburst brooch and earrings

Skill level:

brooch ❖ ❖

earrings ❖

It looks intricate, yet this stunning brooch is created using modular origami pieces based on surprisingly simple folds. In all, 64 pieces are cleverly combined and converted into the shape of a bursting sun.

YOU WILL NEED

Brooch
+ 3 x 5 cm (1¼ x 2 in.) pieces solid-colour washi paper (x 64)
  24 pieces colour **a**
  20 pieces colour **b**
  20 pieces colour **c**
+ 4 cm (1.5 in.) plastic disc
+ 2.5 cm (1 in.) bar pin

Earrings
+ 3 x 5 cm (1¼ x 2 in.) solid-colour washi paper (x 6) 2 pieces each of colour **a**, **b** and **c**
+ 2 beads
+ 2.5 cm (1 in.) eye pin (x 2)
+ 2 fish-hook earring findings

+ glue stick
+ epoxy glue
+ coating material and brush
+ round toothpick to apply glue
+ cutting pliers
+ round-nose pliers

Simple but stunning matching earrings in complementary colours take only minutes to make.

FOLDING INSTRUCTIONS

For the brooch, make 16 Modular Pieces A: eight in colour **a**, four in colour **b** and four in colour **c**. Make all the remaining 48 sheets into Modular Pieces B. The Modular Pieces A, with thicker, more durable corners, are used for the outside row, and Modular Pieces B are used for the inside row, as the corners are thinner and easier to insert into the other pieces. For the earrings, fold six Modular Pieces A. Follow the folding instructions for Modular Pieces (see page 25).

FINISHING THE BROOCH

1 Unfold the triangular flaps of all pieces A, apply glue on the backs of the flaps and fold them back. This step is optional for pieces B.

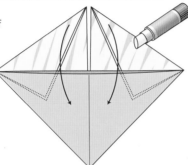

2 Fold all the pieces (both A and B) in half along the middle. Set aside 16 pieces B made with colour **c** for row 1.

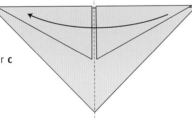

3 Collect 16 pieces B made with colour **b**. Connect the pieces together by inserting a right arm into a right pocket, and a left arm into a left pocket. These pieces are for row 2.

4 Connect 16 pieces B made with colour **a** together as in step 3: these are for row 3.

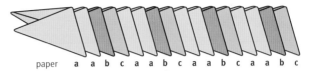

paper **a a b c a a b c a a b c a a b c**

5 Collect 16 pieces A, four made with colour **a**, four with colour **b** and four with colour **c**. Connect these pieces in the colour order **aabc**, as shown. These are for row 4, the outside row.

6 Start assembling the pieces. Position all row 2 pieces with the triangular flaps on the bottom. Take a row 1 piece and insert its left arm into the left pocket of the first piece of row 2. Then insert the right arm of the same row 1 pieces into the right pocket of row 2's second piece. Before inserting the pieces, apply a small amount of epoxy glue to the arm tips.

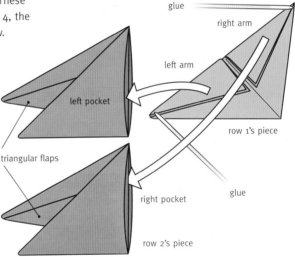

7 Then take another row 1 piece and insert its left arm into the left pocket of row 2's second piece, and its right arm into the right pocket of row 2's third piece. Again, apply a little epoxy glue on the tips of the arms before inserting them.

CONTINUED ON NEXT PAGE ▶

8 Repeat step 7 until all row 1 and row 2 pieces are connected together. At the end, insert the right arm of row 1's last piece into the right pocket of row 2's first piece to form a circle.

9 Now connect row 3 pieces: position them with the triangular flaps on the bottom. Insert one arm each of two row 2 pieces into the pockets of a row 3 piece. Use the tip of a toothpick to apply a small amount of epoxy glue inside the pockets before inserting the arms. Repeat this until all row 3 pieces are connected to row 2 pieces.

row 3's piece

triangular flaps on bottom

10 Repeat step 9 to connect row 4 pieces.

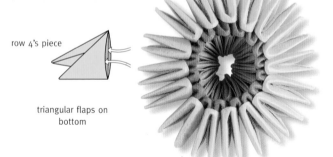

row 4's piece

triangular flaps on bottom

11 When all four rows are connected the brooch is ready for coating. Coat it and let dry completely.

12 Using epoxy glue, place a plastic disc on the back of the brooch, and glue a bar pin on the plastic.

Vivid variations
Experiment with different types and colours of paper. The impressions made by the finished pieces will change drastically.

ASSEMBLING THE EARRINGS

1 Place the colour **b** piece with the triangular flaps on the right side. Bend the end of an eye pin and tuck it under the triangular flap as shown. Then bend the eye pin at the point where it comes out from the flap. Apply epoxy glue under the flap covering the eye pin. Also apply glue inside to fix the right and left arms together.

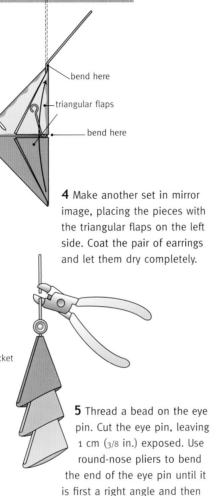

bend here

triangular flaps

bend here

2 Fold one colour **c** and one colour **a** piece in half, positioning them with the triangular flaps on the right side.

colour b

right pocket

colour c

right arm

right pocket

left pocket

left arm

colour a

right arm

left pocket

left arm

3 Connect the colour **c** piece to the colour **b** piece by inserting the right arm into the right pocket, and the left arm into the left pocket. Apply a little epoxy glue inside the pockets before inserting the arms. Repeat this to connect the colour **a** piece to the colour **c** piece.

4 Make another set in mirror image, placing the pieces with the triangular flaps on the left side. Coat the pair of earrings and let them dry completely.

5 Thread a bead on the eye pin. Cut the eye pin, leaving 1 cm (3/8 in.) exposed. Use round-nose pliers to bend the end of the eye pin until it is first a right angle and then a round loop.

6 Attach fish-hook findings to complete the earrings (see page 39).

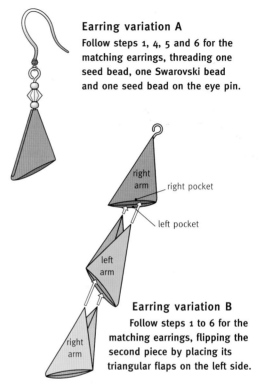

Earring variation A

Follow steps 1, 4, 5 and 6 for the matching earrings, threading one seed bead, one Swarovski bead and one seed bead on the eye pin.

right arm

right pocket

left pocket

left arm

right arm

Earring variation B

Follow steps 1 to 6 for the matching earrings, flipping the second piece by placing its triangular flaps on the left side.

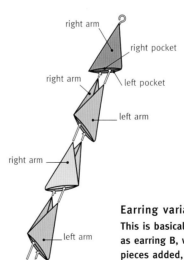

right arm

right pocket

right arm

left pocket

left arm

right arm

left arm

right arm

Earring variation C

This is basically the same as earring B, with two more pieces added, alternating the right-left orientation as shown.

Sweet colours necklace, bracelet and earrings

Skill level: ❖ ❖ ❖

What is your favourite sweet flavour – strawberry, orange, lemon, mint or blueberry? It is hard to pick just one! These beads cheerfully string together all the different colours. Good luck with picking the one colour for matching earrings.

This cute matching necklace and bracelet are basically the same – just vary the size and number of beads used.

YOU WILL NEED

Necklace
+ 4.5 cm (13/4 in.) squares solid-colour washi paper (x 11) 2 blue, 2 light blue, 2 green, 2 yellow, 2 orange and 1 pink
+ 4 mm (1/6 in.) white round beads (x 38)
+ 8 mm (5/16 in.) white round beads (x 12)
+ about 60 cm (24 in.) long fine bead wire
+ toggle clasp

Bracelet
+ 4.5 cm (13/4 in.) squares solid-colour washi paper (x 11) 2 blue, 2 light blue, 2 green, 2 yellow, 2 orange and 1 pink
+ 3 mm (1/8 in.) white round beads (x 6)
+ 6 mm (1/4 in.) white round beads (x 12)
+ about 30 cm (12 in.) length fine bead wire
+ toggle clasp

Earrings
+ 4.5 cm (13/4 in.) squares solid-colour washi paper (colour of your choice) (x 2)
+ 3 mm (1/8 in.) white round beads (x 3)
+ 3 mm (1/8 in.) coloured round beads (x 3)
+ 4 cm (11/2 in.) head pins (x 2)
+ 2 fish-hook earring findings

+ polyester stuffing
+ epoxy glue
+ coating material and brush
+ round toothpick to apply glue
+ beading awl
+ beading needle
+ clear nail polish
+ round-nose pliers
+ cutting pliers

FOLDING INSTRUCTIONS

This project uses Chunky Beads (see page 30). Make the beads using the materials listed.

ASSEMBLING THE NECKLACE

1 Coat all the chunky beads. Before they are dried, while they are still soft, roll them between your fingers to make them rounder.

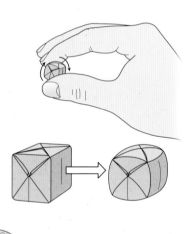

2 Attach the beading wire to the ring of the toggle clasp. Apply clear nail polish to the wire to help secure the end.

3 String nineteen 4 mm (1/6 in.) round beads, then one 8 mm (5/16 in.) round bead.

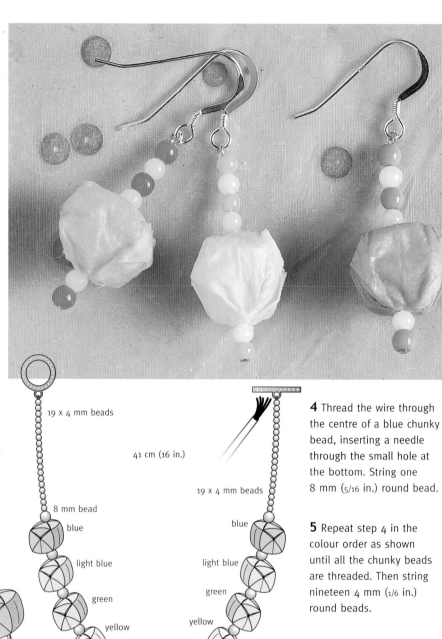

19 x 4 mm beads

41 cm (16 in.)

8 mm bead

blue

light blue

green

yellow

orange

pink

19 x 4 mm beads

blue

light blue

green

yellow

orange

4 Thread the wire through the centre of a blue chunky bead, inserting a needle through the small hole at the bottom. String one 8 mm (5/16 in.) round bead.

5 Repeat step 4 in the colour order as shown until all the chunky beads are threaded. Then string nineteen 4 mm (1/6 in.) round beads.

6 Tie the end of the wire to the T-bar of the toggle clasp and pull the short end of the wire through a few beads. Apply clear nail polish where it is tied.

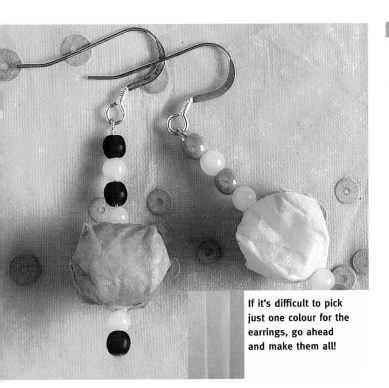

If it's difficult to pick just one colour for the earrings, go ahead and make them all!

ASSEMBLING THE EARRINGS

1 Follow step 1 as for the necklace. Make two pieces.

2 Thread a coloured bead on a head pin, followed by a white bead.

3 Pierce the centre of a chunky bead with a beading awl, and insert the head pin from the bottom up through the hole.

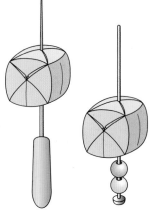

4 Thread a white bead, a coloured bead, a white bead and a coloured bead on the eye pin, then cut the pin, leaving 1 cm (3/8 in.) exposed.

5 Use round-nose pliers to bend the exposed portion of the eye pin into a right angle, then roll it into a round loop. Attach findings to complete the earrings (see page 39).

ASSEMBLING THE BRACELET

1 The bracelet is made in the same way as the necklace, using three 3 mm (1/8 in.) round beads for both ends, and 6 mm (1/4 in.) round beads between chunky beads.

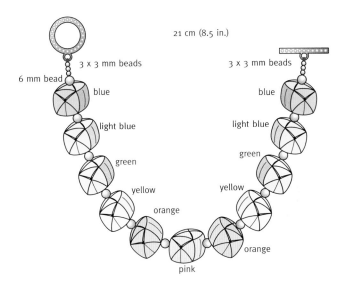

21 cm (8.5 in.)

3 x 3 mm beads

3 x 3 mm beads

6 mm bead

blue

blue

light blue

light blue

green

green

yellow

yellow

orange

orange

pink

Crab brooch and earrings

Skill level:

brooch ❖ ❖ ❖

earrings ❖ ❖ ❖

You can almost feel the sand between your toes when you wear these summery crabs. Their charm will bring a smile to your face even when you are full of winter blues.

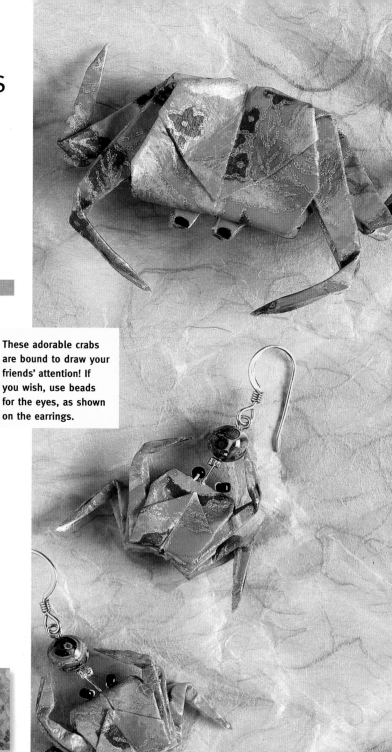

YOU WILL NEED

Brooch

+ 15 cm (6 in.) square yuzen washi paper
+ about 2 x 2.5 cm (3/4 x 1 in.) plastic sheet
+ 2.5 cm (1 in.) bar pin

Earrings

+ 7.5 cm (3 in.) squares yuzen washi paper (x 2)
+ 4 black seed beads
+ 5 mm (1/4 in.) round beads (x 2)
+ 2 crimp beads
+ beading or sewing thread
+ 2.5 cm (1 in.) eye pins (x 2)
+ 2 fish-hook earring findings

+ glue stick
+ epoxy glue
+ coating material and brush
+ round toothpick to apply glue
+ scissors
+ permanent marker
+ sewing needle
+ round-nose pliers
+ cutting pliers
+ crimping pliers

These adorable crabs are bound to draw your friends' attention! If you wish, use beads for the eyes, as shown on the earrings.

FOLDING THE CRAB

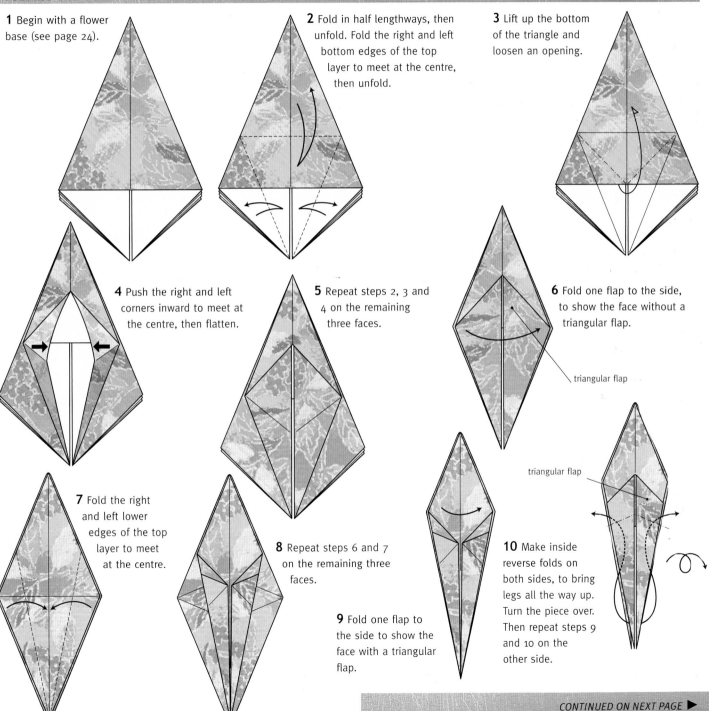

1 Begin with a flower base (see page 24).

2 Fold in half lengthways, then unfold. Fold the right and left bottom edges of the top layer to meet at the centre, then unfold.

3 Lift up the bottom of the triangle and loosen an opening.

4 Push the right and left corners inward to meet at the centre, then flatten.

5 Repeat steps 2, 3 and 4 on the remaining three faces.

6 Fold one flap to the side, to show the face without a triangular flap.

triangular flap

7 Fold the right and left lower edges of the top layer to meet at the centre.

8 Repeat steps 6 and 7 on the remaining three faces.

9 Fold one flap to the side to show the face with a triangular flap.

triangular flap

10 Make inside reverse folds on both sides, to bring legs all the way up. Turn the piece over. Then repeat steps 9 and 10 on the other side.

CONTINUED ON NEXT PAGE ▶

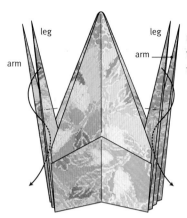

leg   leg
arm   arm
arm

11 Make inside reverse folds on two legs, to fold these legs in half.

12 Fold down the top triangle.

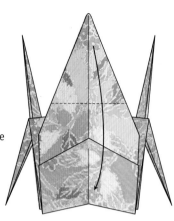

13 Make outside reverse folds on both arms.

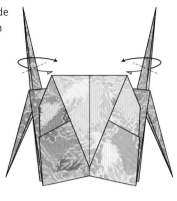

14 Slit the triangle up the middle from the bottom to about half way, then fold the tips of the triangle and tuck them inside the layers.

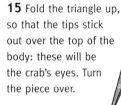

15 Fold the triangle up, so that the tips stick out over the top of the body: these will be the crab's eyes. Turn the piece over.

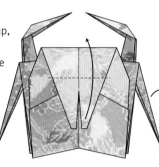

16 The completed crab, ready for attaching jewellery findings.

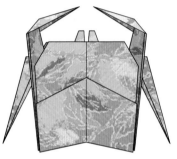

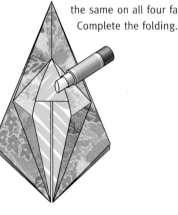

ASSEMBLING THE BROOCH

1 Complete the folding to step 5, then open up the bottom half and, using a glue stick, apply glue inside. Do the same on all four faces. Complete the folding.

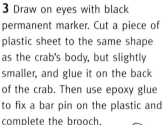

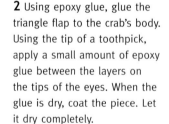

2 Using epoxy glue, glue the triangle flap to the crab's body. Using the tip of a toothpick, apply a small amount of epoxy glue between the layers on the tips of the eyes. When the glue is dry, coat the piece. Let it dry completely.

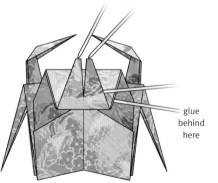

glue behind here

3 Draw on eyes with black permanent marker. Cut a piece of plastic sheet to the same shape as the crab's body, but slightly smaller, and glue it on the back of the crab. Then use epoxy glue to fix a bar pin on the plastic and complete the brooch.

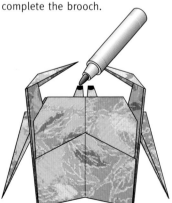

ASSEMBLING THE EARRINGS

1 Follow step 1 for the brooch. Complete the folding to step 13. Make two pieces.

2 Coat the pieces and let dry completely.

3 Lift the triangle flap, then sew two black seed beads to the top of the crab's body. Tie the thread behind the triangle flap.

4 Thread a round bead on an eye pin, then add a crimp bead and crimp it right underneath the round bead.

5 Pierce the crab between the two black seed beads. Insert the eye pin from the top through the hole. Cut off the bottom of the eye pin, leaving about 5 mm (1/4 in.) exposed.

6 Use round-nose pliers to bend the bottom of the eye pin. Apply epoxy glue to secure the eye pin and the thread in place. Then fold down the triangle flap and tuck it under the top layer of the bottom of the crab.

Vivid variations

Bright red is a stunning choice for this project. Temomi (hand-wrinkled) washi paper is used here to give some texture.

7 Turn the piece over. Attach findings to complete the earrings (see page 39).

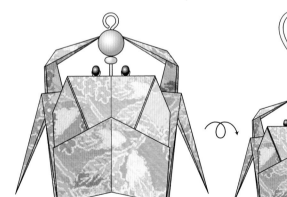

Seashell brooch, necklace and earrings

Skill level:

brooch ❖

necklace ❖

earrings ❖ ❖

Comb the shore for seashells any time of year! Adding beads to the shells rewards your beachcombing with tiny pearls.

YOU WILL NEED

Brooch

+ 11.5 cm (4½ in.) square ivory-colour granite printer paper
+ 1.5 cm (½ in.) round glass or pearl bead
+ about 2 x 4 cm (¾ x 1½ in.) plastic sheet
+ 2.5 cm (1 in.) bar pin

Necklace

+ 11.5 cm (4½ in.) square ivory-colour granite printer paper
+ 10 mm (⅜ in.) round glass or pearl bead
+ about 10 cm (4 in.) length 22-gauge silver wire
+ 2.1 m (84 in.) length hemp

Earrings

+ 4.5 cm (1¾ in.) squares ivory-colour granite printer paper (x 2)
+ 6 mm (¼ in.) round glass or pearl beads, 2 pieces
+ 2 crimp beads
+ 5 cm (2 in.) eye pins (x 2)
+ 2 fish-hook earring findings

+ glue stick
+ epoxy glue
+ coating material and brush
+ round toothpick to apply glue
+ scissors
+ cutting pliers
+ round-nose pliers
+ crimping pliers
+ beading awl

The granite paper and hemp twine give a natural, sandy look.

FOLDING THE SEASHELL

1 Begin with a blintz base (see page 21).

2 Lay the base diagonally and fold it in half sideways, then unfold.

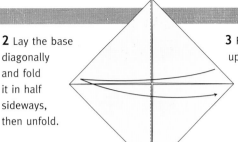

3 Fold in half upwards.

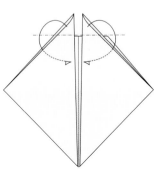

4 Fold the bottom left and right corners up to meet at the top point, then unfold.

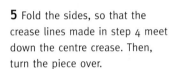

5 Fold the sides, so that the crease lines made in step 4 meet down the centre crease. Then, turn the piece over.

6 Make sure that all the crease lines already made are mountain-folded crease lines. Then make the following valley-folded creases, as shown in the diagram.
Fold A–B to A–D, then unfold.
Fold A–D to A–F, then unfold.
Fold A–C to A–E, then unfold.
Fold A–E to A–F, then unfold.

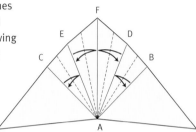

7 Fold down the tip of the top point, folding both layers together.

8 Separate the two layers slightly and fold in the points again, between the layers. Close the layers and turn the piece over.

9 Fold the bottom edges up to meet at the centre.

10 Reverse-fold the points at the top, so that the tips are tucked inside the layers.

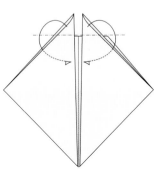

11 Fold the flaps down at an angle outwards, so that they stick out a little at the sides.

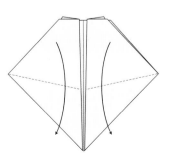

12 Fold up the bottom point to align with the bottoms of the flaps.

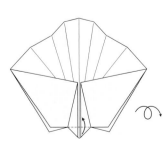

13 Turn the completed piece over.

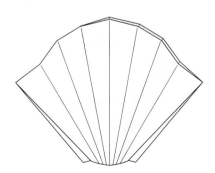

ASSEMBLING THE BROOCH

1 Make a blintz base, then unfold the paper completely. Using a glue stick, apply glue everywhere inside, then refold the blintz base. Let the glue dry completely. Continue folding to step 10.

2 After folding step 10, unfold the piece back to the blintz base, but keep all four corners folded as shown. Apply glue stick to the areas shown. Complete the folding.

3 On the back of the seashell, lift the flaps and apply epoxy glue to the areas shown. When the glue has dried, coat the piece, and let dry completely.

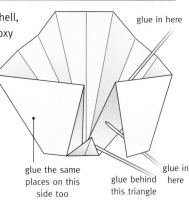

glue in here

glue the same places on this side too

glue behind this triangle

glue in here

4 After coating, the crease lines may not be as clear, so re-crease those on the front layer. Take care to keep the mountain folds and valley folds the same as originally folded.

5 Cut a piece of plastic sheet into the shape shown and use epoxy glue to fix it on the back of the seashell. Then glue the bar pin on the plastic.

6 Glue a bead on the triangle tips in the opening of the seashell to complete the brooch.

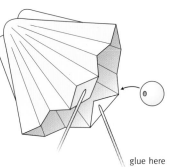

glue here

ASSEMBLING THE NECKLACE

1 Follow steps 1, 2 and 4 for the brooch, coating it after step 2 and leaving it to dry. (Skip step 3.)

2 Make a loop about 5 mm (1/4 in.) in diameter in the middle of the wire. To make a loop, wrap the wire around a thin round dowel, skewer, chopstick, or fine pencil, and twist it to make a loop.

3 Thread a round bead on the wire. Using the tip of a toothpick, apply a small amount of epoxy glue to the bottom of the bead to secure it to the wire.

glue

TOP VIEW
front

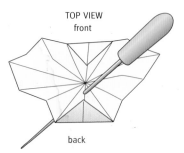

back

4 Use a beading awl to pierce a hole on the centre of the seashell's back, from the inside.

5 Insert the end of the wire from the top through the hole. Cut the ends of the wire, leaving about 1.25 cm (1/2 in.) exposed. Use round-nose pliers to bend the ends of the wire and hide them behind the flaps.

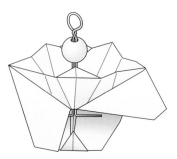

6 On the back of the seashell, lift the flaps and apply epoxy glue to the areas shown. Also apply glue to the ends of the wire, and to the back of the round bead for an extra strength.

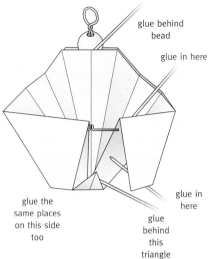

glue behind bead

glue in here

glue the same places on this side too

glue behind this triangle

glue in here

7 Cut the hemp in half. Holding two strands together, fold it in half to find the middle. Make a single knot 2.5 cm (1 in.) away from the middle, then make a single knot 2.5 cm (1 in.) away from the middle to the other side. Make four more single-knots on each side, 5 cm (2 in.) apart. Make one single knot at each end of the hemp.

HOW TO MAKE A SINGLE KNOT

5 cm (2 in.)

5 cm (2 in.)

5 cm (2 in.)

5 cm (2 in.)

2.5 cm. (1 in.)   2.5 cm (1 in.)

centre

8 Insert the hemp through the loop to connect the seashell and complete the necklace. Tie the ends of the hemp together to make the necklace the required length.

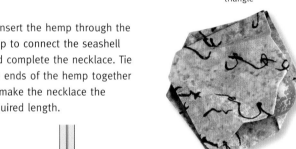

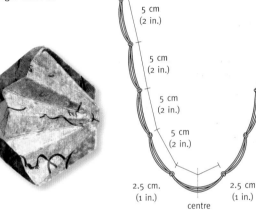

Vivid variations
Yuzen washi patterns make a bolder statement – try matching vivid bead colours too.

ASSEMBLING THE EARRINGS

1 Instead of making a blintz base, start with step 2 of folding the seashell. Make two pieces.

2 Work through to step 10, then unfold the piece completely, except the four corners. Apply glue as shown in step 2 for the brooch. Complete folding.

3 Coat the pieces, let them dry, and then follow step 4 as for the brooch.

4 Thread a round bead and a crimp bead on an eye pin. Crimp the crimp bead to secure the round bead. Follow steps 4, 5 and 6 for the necklace, inserting the eye pin instead of the wire.

5 Attach earring findings to complete the earrings (see page 39).

crimp bead

Leaf brooch and earrings

Skill level:

brooch ❖

earrings ❖

Autumn is many people's favourite season. Bright red, orange and yellow leaves provide plenty of artistic inspiration. The leaf brooch and earrings shown here are made with mujizome (solid-colour) washi paper, dyed with two colours of ink – green and red. The two colours blend with harmony in one sheet of paper to reproduce a beautiful autumnal tint.

YOU WILL NEED

Brooch

- 7.5 x 15 cm (3 x 6 in.) solid-colour washi paper
- about 2.5 x 6.5 cm (1 x 2½ in.) plastic sheet
- 4 cm (1½ in.) bar pin

Earrings

- 4 x 8 cm (1½ x 3 in.) solid-colour washi paper (x 2)
- 2.5 cm (1 in.) eye pins (x 2)
- 2 fish-hook earring findings

- glue stick
- epoxy glue
- coating material and brush
- round toothpick to apply glue
- scissors
- round-nose pliers
- cutting pliers
- beading awl

Vivid variations
Simply adding tiny beads will enhance the elegance of these earrings.

FOLDING THE LEAF

1 Fold in half widthways, then unfold.

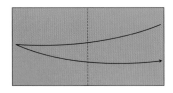

2 Fold the bottom right and left corners up to the middle of the top edge, so that the bottom edges meet down the middle.

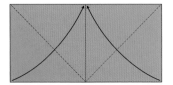

3 Mountain-fold in half lengthways, then unfold.

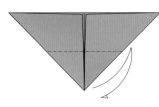

4 Mountain-fold the bottom corner up to the crease of the last fold, then unfold. Mountain-fold the top edge down to meet the same line, then unfold.

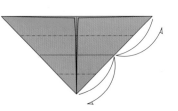

5 Fold the bottom corner up to A–A1.

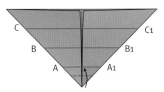

6 Fold A–A1 to meet B–B1. Turn the piece over, then fold B–B1 to C–C1, and C–C1 to the top edge to make a pleat effect.

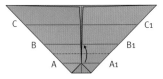

7 Fold the triangle at each end in half.

8 Then fold the triangle at each end down and tuck it under the next triangle.

9 Mountain-fold in half widthways

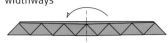

10 To complete the leaf, glue the two sides together with epoxy glue. Pull out the triangle on the fold made in step 9 and pinch the end to form a stem. If you find this difficult, especially working on a small piece, leave this step until brushing with coating, as it is easier to pull out the triangle when the paper is soft. Also, using round-nose pliers may help.

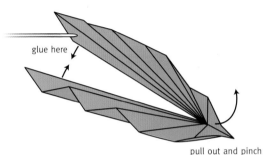

glue here

pull out and pinch the triangle

ASSEMBLING THE BROOCH

1 Complete steps 1 and 2 for folding the leaf, then unfold the paper completely. Using a glue stick, apply glue all over the inside and refold the piece. Let it dry completely, then continue folding to the end of step 8.

2 Unfold the triangles fold in step 8, apply epoxy glue and refold them. Complete the folding, including the gluing in step 10.

glue on this triangle   glue on this triangle

3 Coat the piece and let it dry completely. After coating, the creased lines will not be as sharp but keep them slightly softer, instead of re-creasing the lines, to obtain the rounder shape of the leaf.

4 Cut a piece of plastic sheet to the shape of the leaf, but slightly smaller, and use epoxy glue to fix it on the back of the leaf. Then glue the bar pin on the plastic.

ASSEMBLING THE EARRINGS

1 Follow steps 1 and 2 for the brooch. Before gluing the two sides together at the end of folding, use a beading awl to pierce the centre of the leaf. Take care not to make a hole on the stem (the little triangle pinched out in the last step 10 of folding). Make two pieces.

2 Insert an eye pin through the hole and then glue the two sides together. Apply extra glue on the eye pin to secure it. Let the glue dry, then coat the pieces and let dry completely.

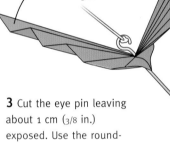

glue

3 Cut the eye pin leaving about 1 cm (3/8 in.) exposed. Use the round-nose pliers to bend the exposed portion of the eye pin into a right angle, then roll it into a loop.

4 Attach fish-hook findings to complete the earrings (see page 39).

These earrings are the perfect example of how two-tone washi paper can bring out rich autumnal hues.

Chunky bead choker and earrings

Skill level: ❖ ❖ ❖

It may be hard to believe, but these beads are the same as those used for the Sweet Colours Necklace (see page 70). A combination of artistic yuzen washi paper and carefully chosen bead caps transform the chunky beads into elegant jewellery.

YOU WILL NEED

Choker

+ 4 cm (1½ in.) squares yuzen washi paper (x 7)
+ 1 cm (3/8 in.) bead caps (x 7)
+ 4 cm (1½ in.) head pins (x 5)
+ 4 cm (1½ in.) eye pins (x 2)
+ 8 mm (5/16 in.) round beads (x 48)
+ about 45 cm (18 in.) length beading wire
+ 1 jewellery clasp
+ 1 split ring
+ 2 crimp beads

Earrings

+ 4 cm (1½ in.) squares yuzen washi paper (x 2)
+ 1 cm (3/8 in.) bead caps (x 2)
+ 4 cm (1½ in.) head pins (x 2)
+ 2 fish-hook earring findings

+ polyester stuffing
+ epoxy glue
+ coating material and brush
+ round toothpick to apply glue
+ beading awl
+ cutting pliers
+ round-nose pliers
+ crimping pliers

Replace bead caps with beads of your choice. Alternate with different types, patterns and colours of paper.

FOLDING INSTRUCTIONS

Make the beads following the instructions for Chunky Beads (see page 30), using the materials listed here.

ASSEMBLING THE CHOKER

1 Coat the chunky beads and let them dry. Pierce the centre of each bead with a beading awl.

2 Insert a head pin from the bottom through the hole. Thread a bead cap on the pin over the bead. Use the tip of a toothpick to apply a small amount of epoxy glue between the pin head and bead, and under the bead cap. Cut the pin, leaving 1 cm (3/8 in.) exposed.

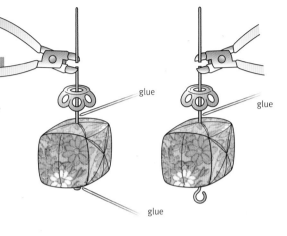

glue

glue

glue

3 Use round-nose pliers to bend the pin into a right angle, then roll it into a loop.

4 Repeat steps 2 and 3 on four more beads.

5 Repeat steps 2 and 3 on two more beads, using an eye pin instead of a head pin.

6 Connect two beads with eye pins vertically, and one bead with a head pin on the bottom.

7 String 18 round beads on wire, then thread the beads as follows:
1 chunky bead with head pin
3 round beads
  1 chunky bead with head pin
    3 round beads
      the 3 connected
        chunky beads

3 round beads
1 chunky bead with head pin
3 round beads
1 chunky bead with head pin
18 round beads.

8 Attach a clasp at one end of the wire and a split ring on the other end, using crimp beads.

ASSEMBLING THE EARRINGS

1 Follow steps 1 to 3 for the choker, preparing two beads. Then attach fish-hook earring findings (see page 39).

37.5 cm
(15 in.)

Shades of autumn necklace and earrings

Skill level: ❖

Select your favourite autumnal shades for this necklace, which is made with simple modular pieces, easily connected, and finished with leather cords. The matching earrings take only minutes to make. Vary the colours to create shades of another season.

"Simple" and "elegant" are the perfect words to describe this stunning necklace.

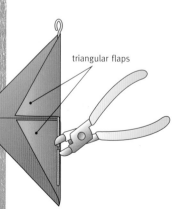

YOU WILL NEED

Necklace

+ 3 x 5 cm (1¼ x 2 in.) solid-colour washi paper (x 17)
  5 each in colours **a**, **b** and **c**
  1 piece each in colours **d** and **e**
+ 12.5 cm (5 in.) lengths, 2 mm (⅛ in.) diameter leather cord (x 2)
+ jewellery clasp
+ 7 mm (5/16 in.) split ring
+ 5 mm (¼ in.) split ring
+ 2 fold-over connectors
+ 2.5 cm (1 in.) eye pins (x 3)

Earrings

+ 3 x 5 cm (1¼ x 2 in.) solid-colour washi paper (x 6)
  2 each in colour **a**, **b** and **c**
+ 2.5 cm (1 in.) eye pins (x 2)
+ 2 fish-hook earring findings

+ epoxy glue
+ coating material and brush
+ round toothpick to apply glue
+ cutting pliers
+ round-nose pliers

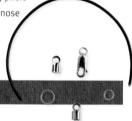

FOLDING INSTRUCTIONS

Modular Pieces A (see page 25) are used for this project. Paper size, numbers and colours are listed here.

ASSEMBLING THE NECKLACE

1 Take one colour **a** piece, with the triangular flaps on the right side, and tuck an eye pin under the flap as shown. Cut the end of the eye pin, leaving 1 cm (3/8 in.) exposed.

2 Use round-nose pliers to bend the exposed end of the eye pin, and also to bend just underneath the eye of the eye pin. Apply epoxy glue under the flap covering the eye pin. Also apply glue inside to fix the right and left arms together.

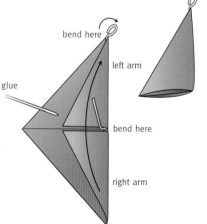

triangular flaps

bend here

left arm

glue

bend here

right arm

3 Take one piece in colour **a**, two pieces in colour **b** and two pieces in colour **c**. Position them with the triangular flaps on the right side, and fold in half.

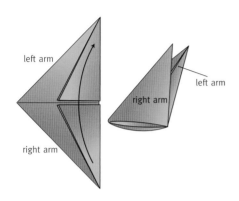

left arm

left arm

right arm

right arm

4 Using the tip of a toothpick, apply a small amount of epoxy glue into the pockets of the piece with the eye pin attached. Then insert the right arm of a colour **b** piece into the right pocket of the piece with the eye pin, and the left arm into the left pocket. Insert only the tips of the arms.

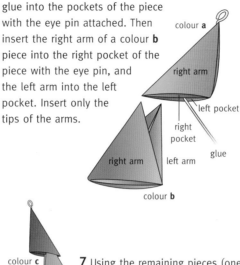

colour **a**

right arm

left pocket

right pocket

glue

right arm

left arm

colour **b**

5 Repeat step 4 with the other four pieces folded in half in step 3, in the colour order as shown. When connecting pieces, tilt each piece a little so that the strand is slightly curved.

colour **a**

colour **b**

colour **c**

colour **a**

colour **b**

colour **c**

6 Repeat steps 1 to 5 to make another strand with the same number and colour arrangement of pieces, but place all the pieces with the triangular flaps on the left side.

colour **a**

colour **b**

colour **c**

colour **a**

colour **b**

colour **c**

colour **c**

colour **d**

colour **b**

colour **a**

colour **e**

7 Using the remaining pieces (one of each colour), repeat steps 1 to 5 to make one more strand. Place the pieces with the triangular flaps on the left side and connect them in a straight line.

8 Coat all three strands and let them dry completely. Attach the eye pin of each strand to a 1/4 in. (5 mm) jump ring as shown.

9 Using the tip of a toothpick, apply epoxy glue inside the pockets of the end pieces and insert the ends of the leather cords. Attach the clasp pieces to the other ends of the cords.

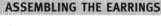

glue

ASSEMBLING THE EARRINGS

1 Make a strand, just like the one in step 7 for the necklace, using three pieces (instead of five), as shown.

2 Make another strand in a mirror image, placing the triangular flaps on the right side for this one. Coat the pieces and let them dry completely. Attach fish-hook findings to finish the earrings (see page 39).

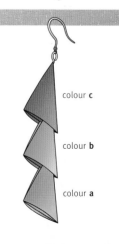

colour **c**

colour **b**

colour **a**

Pumpkin brooch

Skill level: ❖ ❖

The pumpkin, stem and vine are all made from one piece of paper, which involves lots of folds, so choose a thin paper. The finished piece shown here is made with a muji-mara-zome (unevenly dyed solid colour) washi paper to give some depth. Thin mulberry paper is a perfect alternative.

YOU WILL NEED

- ✦ 12.5 cm (5 in.) square solid-colour washi paper
- ✦ about 2.5 x 4 cm (1 x 1½ in.) plastic sheet
- ✦ 4 cm (1½ in.) bar pin
- ✦ epoxy glue
- ✦ coating material and brush
- ✦ round toothpick to apply glue

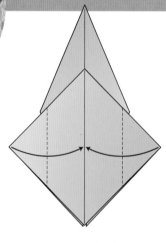

Glue black paper cutouts on the pumpkin before coating to give it a Halloween face.

FOLDING THE PUMPKIN

1 Make a bird base (see page 24), following the instructions to step 5. Turn the piece over.

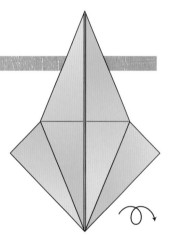

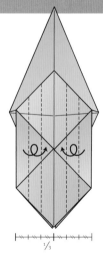

2 Fold both corners to meet at the centre.

3 Roll in one-third on both sides.

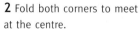

⅓

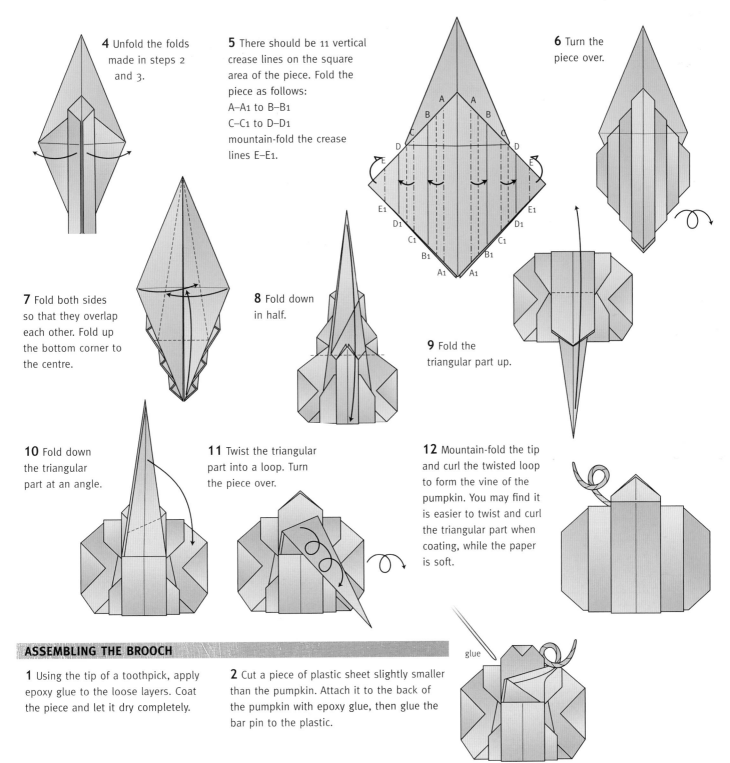

4 Unfold the folds made in steps 2 and 3.

5 There should be 11 vertical crease lines on the square area of the piece. Fold the piece as follows:
A–A1 to B–B1
C–C1 to D–D1
mountain-fold the crease lines E–E1.

6 Turn the piece over.

7 Fold both sides so that they overlap each other. Fold up the bottom corner to the centre.

8 Fold down in half.

9 Fold the triangular part up.

10 Fold down the triangular part at an angle.

11 Twist the triangular part into a loop. Turn the piece over.

12 Mountain-fold the tip and curl the twisted loop to form the vine of the pumpkin. You may find it is easier to twist and curl the triangular part when coating, while the paper is soft.

ASSEMBLING THE BROOCH

1 Using the tip of a toothpick, apply epoxy glue to the loose layers. Coat the piece and let it dry completely.

2 Cut a piece of plastic sheet slightly smaller than the pumpkin. Attach it to the back of the pumpkin with epoxy glue, then glue the bar pin to the plastic.

glue

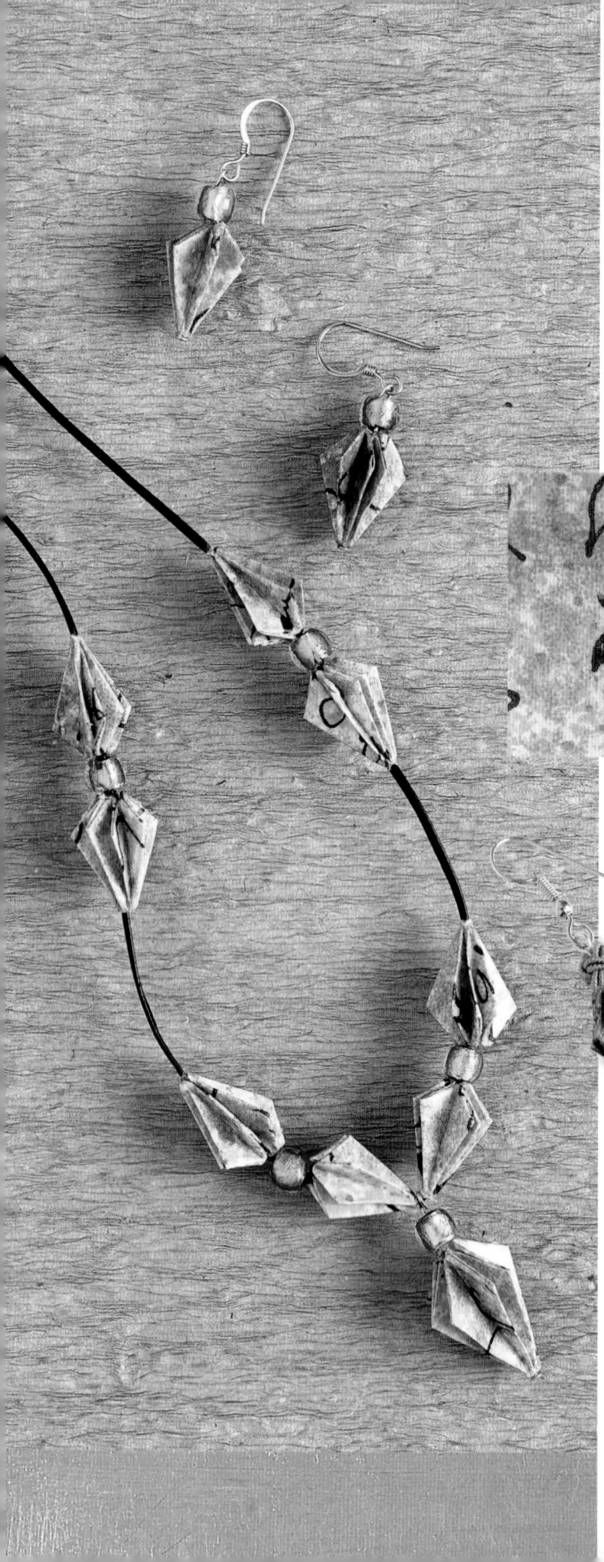

Pinecone necklace and earrings

Skill level:

necklace ❖ ❖ ❖

earrings ❖ ❖ ❖

Using pretty pinecone beads, accented with glass foil beads, on black leather cord creates a unique harmony of materials and textures in this beautiful necklace. Yuzen washi paper is recommended for this piece, since most other materials will not easily fold into these tiny, intricate beads. The yuzen kimono patterns add an artistic touch to the finished work.

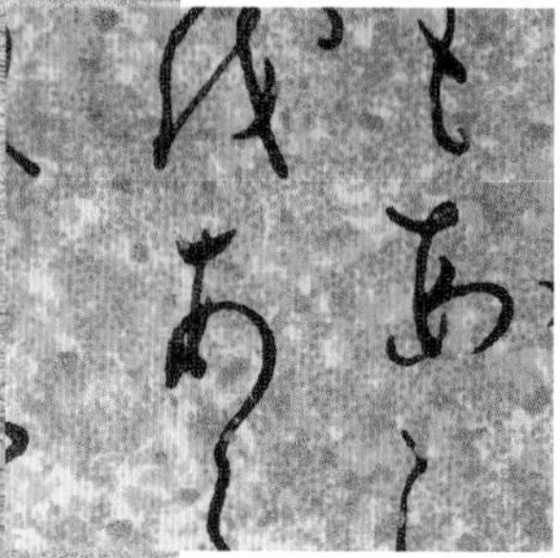

YOU WILL NEED

Necklace

+ yuzen washi paper
  4 cm (1½ in.) squares (x 8)
  5 cm (2 in.) square
+ 6 to 8 mm (¼ to 5/16 in.) glass foil beads (x 5)
+ 5 cm (2 in.) head pin
+ 76 cm (30 in.) length, 1 mm diameter leather cord
+ 1 jewellery clasp
+ 1 split ring
+ 2 fold-over connectors

Earrings

+ yuzen washi paper
  4 cm (1½ in.) squares (x 2)
+ 6 to 8 mm (¼ to 5/16 in.) glass foil beads (x 2)
+ 5 cm (2 in.) head pins (x 2)
+ 2 fish-hook earring findings

+ epoxy glue
+ coating material and brush
+ round toothpick to apply glue
+ beading awl
+ round-nose pliers
+ scissors
+ cutting pliers

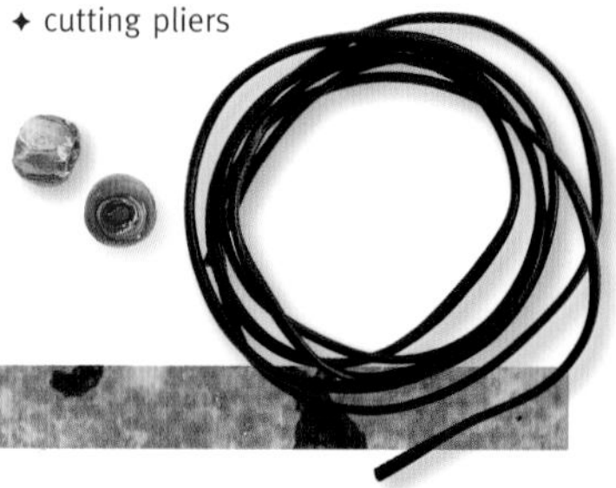

This lovely refined necklace is perfect for special occasions.

FOLDING INSTRUCTIONS

Fold Pinecone Beads (see page 32) for this project, using the materials and quantities listed here.

ASSEMBLING THE NECKLACE

1 Coat the pinecone beads and let them dry.

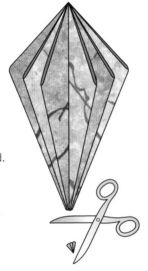

2 Cut off a very small tip from each of the eight beads made with 4 cm (1½ in.) square paper. These will be the beads strung to the cord.

3 Make a charm using the bead made with 5 cm (2 in.) square paper: using a beading awl, pierce the bead centre.

4 Insert a head pin from the bottom. Using the tip of a toothpick, apply a small amount of epoxy glue to the little opening on the top. Squeeze and close the opening with your fingers to secure the head pin.

5 Add a glass foil bead and trim the head pin, leaving 1 cm (3/8 in.) exposed. Using round-nose pliers, bend the end of the pin at a right angle, and then shape it into a loop.

Vivid variations
Changing the size and shape of the beads can transform pinecones into lanterns or umbrellas.

CONTINUED ON NEXT PAGE ▶

6 String the cord as follows:
1 origami bead
1 glass bead
1 origami bead
the origami charm
1 origami bead
1 glass bead
1 origami bead.

7 Centre the set of beads on the cord. Using the tip of a toothpick, apply a small amount of epoxy glue in the openings of the origami beads. Squeeze and close the openings with your fingers, and let the glue dry.

8 On one side of the cord, string one origami bead, one glass bead and one origami bead. Position this set of beads, about 2.5 cm (1 in.) away from the centre set of beads. Apply a small amount of epoxy glue, as in step 7, to keep them in place. Thread the other side of the necklace to match.

9 Attach the clasp pieces at the ends of the cord to finish the necklace.

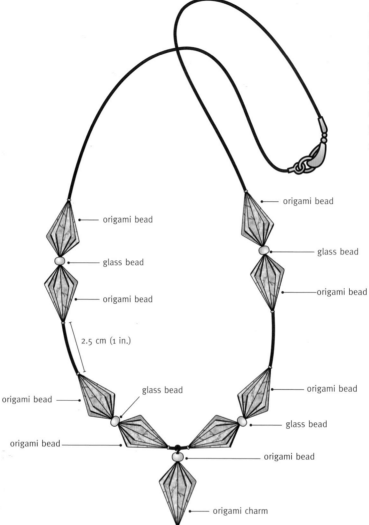

origami bead
glass bead
origami bead
2.5 cm (1 in.)
origami bead
glass bead
origami bead
origami bead
glass bead
origami bead
origami bead
origami bead
glass bead
origami bead
origami charm

Vivid variations
Red-based yuzen washi paper with red and green beads have transformed the look of the pinecones, making the piece ideal for warm winter holidays.

ASSEMBLING THE EARRINGS

1 Make the two pinecone beads, coat them and let them dry completely.

2 Follow steps 3 to 5 for the necklace to make these beads into charms. Attach earring findings to complete (see page 39).

Tree brooch, earrings and pin

Skill level:

brooch ❖

earrings ❖

pin ❖

These trees are simple to make and a fun way to spread a little Christmas cheer. Adding a star-shaped bead completes the tree, or you can add bright beads for a fun finish.

YOU WILL NEED

Brooch

- 5 x 7.5 cm (2 x 3 in.) pieces solid-colour washi paper (x 7), 6 green and 1 brown
- star-shaped bead
- beading or sewing thread
- about 2.5 x 5 cm (1 x 2 in.) plastic sheet
- 2.5 cm (1 in.) bar pin

Earrings

- 3 x 5 cm (1¼ x 2 in.) pieces solid-colour washi paper (x 10), 8 green and 2 brown
- 2 star-shaped beads
- 2.5 cm (1 in.) eye pins (x 2)
- 2 fish-hook earring findings

Pin

- 3 x 5 cm (1¼ x 2 in.) pieces solid-colour washi paper (x 15), 8 light green, 4 dark green and 3 brown
- 3 star-shaped beads
- 2.5 cm (1 in.) eye pins (x 3)
- 4 cm (1½ in.) head pins (x 2)
- 5 mm (¼ in.) jump rings (x 5)
- 5 green round beads
- 5 red round beads
- 10 gold seed beads
- kilt pin with 5 loops

- epoxy glue
- coating material and brush
- round toothpick
- scissors
- sewing needle
- cutting pliers
- round-nose pliers

Add your favourite star-shaped beads to the treetops for a festive finishing touch.

FOLDING INSTRUCTIONS

Modular Pieces A are used for these projects. The paper size, numbers and colours are listed here. Follow the folding instructions for modular pieces (see page 25).

ASSEMBLING THE BROOCH

1 Place three green pieces with triangular flaps on the right, and fold in half. These will be the first, third and fifth pieces. Position three other green pieces with triangular flaps on the left, and fold in half. These will be the second, fourth and sixth pieces.

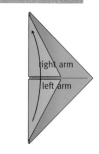

left arm / right arm

right arm / left arm

2 Position the brown piece with triangular flaps on the left, fold in half widthways, then fold in half lengthways.

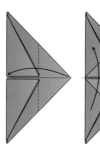

1st piece (triangle flap on right side)

right arm

right pocket

left pocket

right arm

2nd piece (triangle flap on left side)

left arm

3 Using the tip of a toothpick, apply a small amount of epoxy glue in the pockets of the first piece. Then insert the left arm of the second piece into the right pocket of the first piece, and the right arm of the second piece into the left pocket of the first piece.

4 Repeat step 3 with four more green pieces, alternating the right and left orientation as shown. Insert the brown piece into the last green piece, first using a toothpick to apply a small amount of epoxy glue in the pockets.

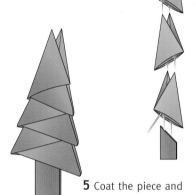

5 Coat the piece and let it dry completely.

6 Sew a star-shaped bead to the top of the tree. Tie the ends of the string between the left and right arms of the first piece. Glue the arms together with epoxy glue.

glue here

7 Cut a piece of plastic sheet to the same shape as the tree, but slightly smaller, and use epoxy glue to stick it on the back. Then glue a bar pin on the plastic.

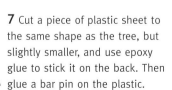

ASSEMBLING THE EARRINGS

1 Make two trees. Before assembling the trees, attach an eye pin to the first piece. Bend the top of an eye pin and tuck it under the triangular flap, as shown. Apply epoxy glue under the triangle flap by the pin and inside the piece to glue the right and left arms together.

2 Assemble the trees as for the brooch, using only four green pieces (instead of six) for each tree. Coat them and let them dry completely.

3 Thread a star-shaped bead on the eye pin. Cut the eye pin leaving 1 cm (3/8 in.) exposed. Use round-nose pliers to bend the exposed portion of pin into a right angle, then roll it into a loop. Attach fish-hook findings to complete the earrings.

ASSEMBLING THE PIN

1 Make three trees as for the earring: two with light green paper and one with dark green paper.

2 Thread a head pin with a red bead, gold seed bead, green bead and gold seed bead. Repeat this pattern once more, then add one red bead, and a gold seed bead.

3 Cut the head pin leaving 3/8 in. (1 cm) exposed. Use round-nose pliers to bend the exposed portion of the eye pin into a right angle, then roll it into a loop.

4 Make another set of beads, this time starting with a green bead, and using three green beads, and two red beads.

5 Attach a jump ring to the trees and the two head pins with beads. Connect them to the kilt pin as shown below.

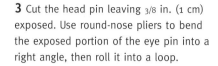

These pieces are made with Japanese throwing stars and accented with star-shaped pewter beads.

Star brooch and earrings

Skill level:
brooch ❖ ❖
earrings ❖ ❖

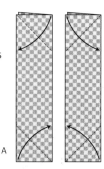

Let these stars brighten the day the way real stars brighten the night. White and gold paper, accented with a star-shaped bead, makes them twinkle.

YOU WILL NEED

Brooch
+ 10 cm (4 in.) square (x 2) and 7.5 cm (3 in.) square (x 2) yuzen washi paper
+ star-shaped bead
+ beading or sewing thread
+ 2.5 cm (1 in.) plastic disc
+ 2.5 cm (1 in.) bar pin

Earrings
+ 5 cm (2 in.) squares yuzen washi paper (x 4)
+ 2 star-shaped beads
+ beading or sewing thread

+ 2.5 cm (1 in.) eye pins (x 2)
+ 2 fish-hook earring findings

+ epoxy glue
+ coating material and brush
+ round toothpick to apply glue
+ sewing needle
+ scissors
+ round-nose pliers
+ cutting pliers

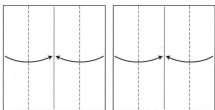

FOLDING THE STAR

1 Take two pieces of the same size. Fold them in half widthways, then unfold.

2 Fold both edges to the centre crease.

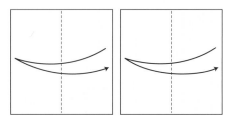

3 Fold in half widthways.

4 Fold down the top and bottom corners in different directions.

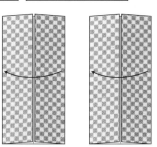

A   B

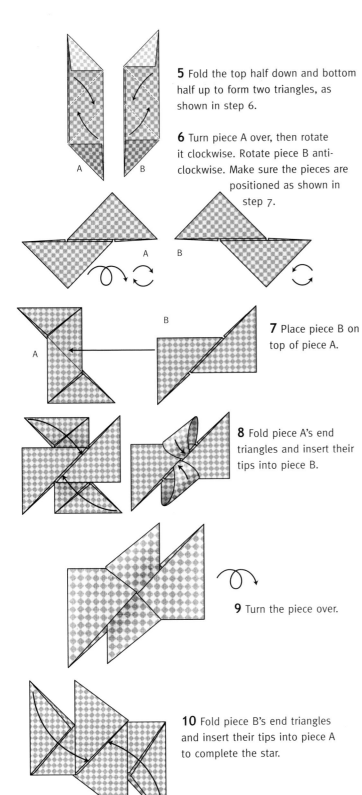

5 Fold the top half down and bottom half up to form two triangles, as shown in step 6.

6 Turn piece A over, then rotate it clockwise. Rotate piece B anti-clockwise. Make sure the pieces are positioned as shown in step 7.

7 Place piece B on top of piece A.

8 Fold piece A's end triangles and insert their tips into piece B.

9 Turn the piece over.

10 Fold piece B's end triangles and insert their tips into piece A to complete the star.

ASSEMBLING THE BROOCH

1 Make two stars in two sizes. Coat and let dry.

2 Place the smaller star on top of the larger one. Insert a threaded needle from the back of the larger star, pull the thread through the centre, thread on the smaller star, and a star-shaped bead, then thread back through the centre of both stars. Tie the thread ends at the back.

3 Apply epoxy glue between the bead and the smaller star, and between the smaller and the larger stars. Glue a plastic disc on the back of the star, then glue a bar pin on the plastic.

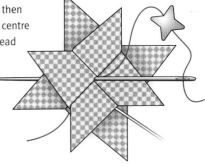

ASSEMBLING THE EARRINGS

1 Make two stars. In step 10 of folding, insert only one triangular tip. Coat the pieces and let dry.

2 Follow step 2 for the brooch, making one star for each earring.

3 Trim an eye pin to 2 cm (3/4 in.). Bend the bottom until it forms a right angle, and also bend a little just beneath the eye of the pin.

4 Place the eye pin under the triangular flap that was not inserted in step 1. Apply a small amount of epoxy glue to the triangular flap and then insert its tip. Make sure the ends of the threads are hidden.

5 Attach earring findings to complete.

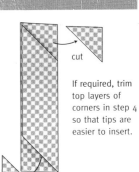

cut

If required, trim top layers of corners in step 4 so that tips are easier to insert.

cut

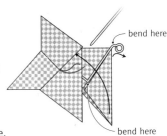

bend here

bend here

Festive foil beaded necklace and earrings

Skill level:

necklace ❖ ❖

earrings ❖ ❖

A variation on chunky beads, these beads are strung with shiny foil beads and little clear blue round ones. Foil gives a subtle, but bright and festive look, which is complemented by snowflake-like charms, made with shiny opalescent paper. Foil and opalescent paper are not suitable for coating, but they are relatively durable.

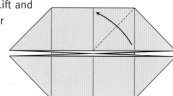

YOU WILL NEED

Necklace

+ 4 cm (1½ in.) squares (x 14) and one 5cm (2 in.) square foil origami paper
+ 5 cm (2 in.) square opalescent origami paper
+ 5 mm (¼ in.) long glass rectangular beads (x 104)
+ 3 mm (⅛ in.) glass round beads (x 55)
+ 5 cm (2 in.) head pin
+ 60 cm (24 in.) and 50 cm (20 in.) lengths fine beading wire
+ 4 crimp beads
+ 2 double-strand end bars
+ 5 mm (¼ in.) split ring
+ 8 mm (5/16 in.) split ring
+ lobster clasp

Earrings A

+ 4 cm (1½ in.) squares foil origami paper (x 2)
+ 3 mm (⅛ in.) glass round beads (x 4)
+ 4 cm (1½ in.) head pins (x 2)
+ 2 fish-hook earring findings

Earrings B

+ 5 cm (2 in.) squares opalescent origami paper (x 2)
+ 5 mm (¼ in.) long glass rectangular beads (x 4)
+ 3 mm (⅛ in.) glass round beads (x 6)
+ 4 cm (1½ in.) eye pins (x 2)
+ 2 fish-hook earring findings

+ glue stick
+ epoxy glue
+ round toothpick
+ beading awl
+ round-nose pliers
+ crimping pliers
+ cutting pliers

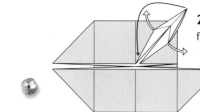

FOLDING INSTRUCTIONS

Chunky Beads are used for this project but they are not filled with polyester stuffing. Follow the folding instructions for Chunky Beads to step 9 (see page 30).

For the necklace, make 14 chunky beads with 4 cm (1½ in.) square foil paper, and one with 5 cm (2 in.) square foil paper. You also need to make one charm with 5 cm (2 in.) square opalescent paper.

For earrings A, you need to make two chunky beads with 4 cm (1½ in.) square foil. For earring B, you need to make two charms with 5 cm (2 in.) square opalescent paper.

ASSEMBLING THE NECKLACE

1 To make a charm for the longer strand, fold a 5 cm (2 in.) square of opalescent paper into a boat base (see page 23). Lift and let the triangular flap stand.

2 Open and flatten the triangular flap to form a square flap.

3 Do the same with the three other triangular flaps to form square flaps.

4 Unfold the piece and apply glue (from a glue stick) to the four corner areas as shown. Then fold it back as in step 3.

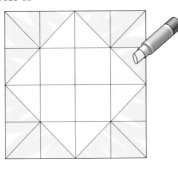

5 Using round-nose pliers, curl both corners of all four square flaps.

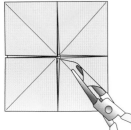

6 Using a beading awl, pierce the back of one of the curled squares. This charm is now ready to be strung.

triangular pocket

7 Make 14 chunky beads (page 30) with 4 cm (1½ in.) foil paper, without using stuffing. Fold the flaps to the side, to show the face without triangular pockets.

8 Pierce the centre of the beads with a beading awl from a small hole on the bottom.

9 To make a charm for the shorter strand, fold a chunky bead with 5 cm (2 in.) foil paper, following steps 7 and 8. Insert a head pin from the bottom up through the hole. Apply a small amount of epoxy glue between the pin's head and the bead. Thread a round bead on the eye pin, then cut the pin leaving 1 cm (3/8 in.) exposed. Use round-nose pliers to bend the pin into a right angle, then roll it into a loop.

glue

This double-strand necklace is great for winter celebrations. Turn to the next page for matching earrings.

CONTINUED ON NEXT PAGE ▶

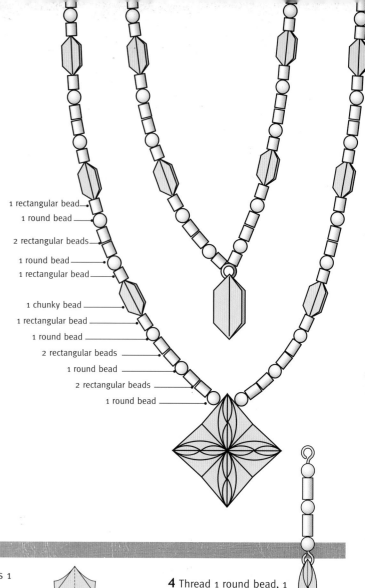

10 String the longer length of beading wire with 1 round bead, 2 rectangular beads, 1 round bead, 2 rectangular beads, 1 round bead and 1 rectangular bead.

11 Then add 1 chunky bead, 1 rectangular bead, 1 round bead, 2 rectangular beads, 1 round bead and 1 rectangular bead. Repeat this step three more times.

12 String the charm made with opalescent paper from the other end of the wire, and centre the charm. Repeat steps 10 and 11 on the other side of the necklace to match.

13 Add 1 rectangular bead on both ends. Then thread both ends with a repeated 1 round bead and 2 rectangular beads pattern until the necklace is about 50 cm (20 in.) long (or as long as you wish).

14 Thread the shorter beading wire with 1 rectangular bead, 1 round bead, 2 rectangular beads, 1 round bead, 1 rectangular bead and 1 chunky bead. Repeat this step twice more.

15 String the charm made with the chunky bead from the other end of the wire, and centre the charm. Repeat step 14 on the other side of the necklace to match. Add 1 rectangular bead and finish threading the ends with 1 round bead followed by 2 rectangular beads until the necklace is about 40 cm (16 in.) long or to your required length.

16 Connect the ends of the wires to the double-strand end bars, securing them with crimping beads. Attach a clasp on one end and the split ring on the other.

1 rectangular bead
1 round bead
2 rectangular beads
1 round bead
1 rectangular bead
1 chunky bead
1 rectangular bead
1 round bead
2 rectangular beads
1 round bead
2 rectangular beads
1 round bead

ASSEMBLING EARRINGS A

1 Make two chunky beads. Follow steps 7 to 9, but without gluing the head pin to the bead. String one round bead on the head pin before inserting the chunky bead. Attach earring findings to complete.

ASSEMBLING EARRINGS B

1 Make two pieces, following steps 1 to 6 for the necklace.

2 Apply epoxy glue on the back of the piece and glue A to A1, B to B1, C to C1, and D to D1. Pinch the corners together until the glue dries.

3 Insert the eye of an eye pin through the hole made in step 6. Apply a small amount of epoxy glue where the eye pin is attached for extra strength.

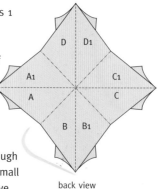

back view

4 Thread 1 round bead, 1 rectangular bead, 1 round bead, 1 rectangular bead and 1 round bead on the pin, then cut it, leaving 1 cm (3/8 in.) exposed. Use round-nose pliers to bend the exposed portion of the head pin into a right angle, then roll it into a loop. Attach earring findings.

Foil gives a shimmering
finish that really
sets off your origami
jewellery and gives a
feminine touch.

Wreath brooch

Skill level: ❖

Simple folds and assembly can give a stunning result. For this striking wreath, keep connecting modular pieces until they form a circle. Add a bright red bow or a star for festive cheer.

YOU WILL NEED

- 3 x 5 cm (1¼ x 2 in.) pieces light green solid-colour washi paper (x 9)
- 3 x 5 cm (1¼ x 2 in.) dark green solid-colour washi paper (x 9)
- 1.5 x 5 cm (½ x 2 in.) pieces (x 2), 1.5 x 6.5 cm (½ x 2½ in.) piece, and 1.5 x 2.5 cm (½ x 1 in.) piece red solid-colour washi paper
- about 1.5 x 2.5 cm (½ x 1 in.) plastic sheet
- 2.5 cm (1 in.) bar pin

- epoxy glue
- glue stick
- coating material and brush
- round toothpick to apply glue
- scissors

FOLDING INSTRUCTIONS

Make nine Modular Pieces A in light green and nine in dark green (see page 25).

ASSEMBLING THE WREATH

1 Fold all 18 modular pieces in half, placing the triangular flaps on top.

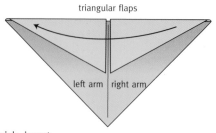

2 Using the tip of a toothpick, insert a small amount of epoxy glue into the pockets of the first piece. Tilt the second piece at an angle of about 20 degrees, then insert the right arm of the second piece into the right pocket of the first piece, and the left arm of the second piece into the left pocket of the first piece.

3 Repeat step 2 with the other 16 pieces, alternating the light green and dark green pieces.

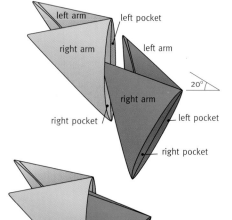

4 After the 18th piece is inserted, insert the right arm of the first piece into the right pocket of the 18th piece, and the left arm of the first piece into the left pocket of the 18th piece to form a circle.

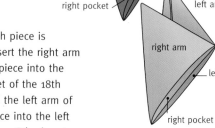

5 To make a bow, fold all four red pieces in half lengthways. Unfold them and use a glue stick to apply glue all over the inside, then fold in half again.

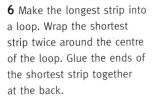

6 Make the longest strip into a loop. Wrap the shortest strip twice around the centre of the loop. Glue the ends of the shortest strip together at the back.

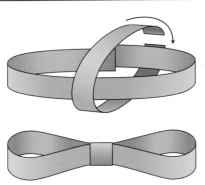

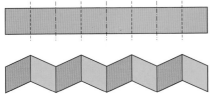

7 Pleat the two remaining strips. Coat all the pieces, including all the red pieces and the wreath. Let dry completely.

The star in the centre of the wreath is the same star shown for the earrings and brooch on page 96.

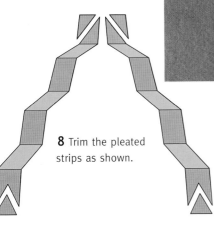

8 Trim the pleated strips as shown.

9 Use epoxy glue to glue the pleated strips and the bow on the upper portion of the wreath.

10 Glue a piece of plastic sheet across the top of the back of the wreath. Then glue a bar pin on the plastic to complete the brooch.

Angel pin and earrings

Skill level:

pin ❖ ❖

earrings ❖ ❖

Never be without your guardian angel when you wear these lovely earrings and pin. Shimmering gold angels are shown here, but you could try angelic white or shiny silver to create your own version.

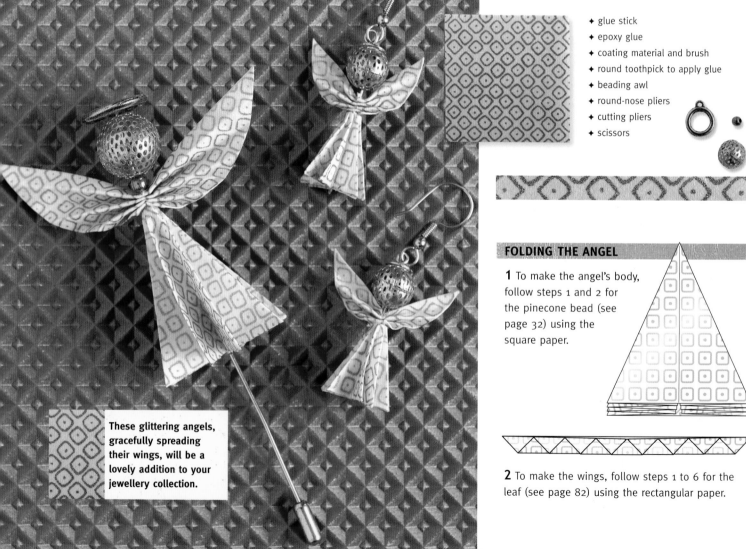

These glittering angels, gracefully spreading their wings, will be a lovely addition to your jewellery collection.

Pin

- ✦ 7.5 cm (3 in.) square and 4 x 7.5 cm (1½ x 3 in.) piece yuzen washi paper
- ✦ 15 mm (5/8 in.) round bead
- ✦ 3 mm (1/8 in.) bead
- ✦ 4 cm (1½ in.) eye pin
- ✦ toggle clasp ring
- ✦ about 2.5 x 4 cm (1 x 1½ in.) plastic sheet

- ✦ 7.5 cm (3 in.) stick pin with 8 mm (5/16 in.) pad

Earrings

- ✦ 4 cm (1½ in.) squares (x 2) and 2 x 4 cm (3/4 x 1½ in.) pieces yuzen washi paper (x 2)
- ✦ 1 cm (3/8 in.) round beads (x 2)
- ✦ 4 cm (1½ in.) eye pins (x 2)
- ✦ 5 mm (1/4 in.) split rings (x 2)
- ✦ 2 fish-hook earring findings

- ✦ glue stick
- ✦ epoxy glue
- ✦ coating material and brush
- ✦ round toothpick to apply glue
- ✦ beading awl
- ✦ round-nose pliers
- ✦ cutting pliers
- ✦ scissors

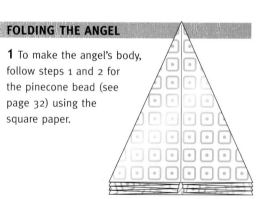

FOLDING THE ANGEL

1 To make the angel's body, follow steps 1 and 2 for the pinecone bead (see page 32) using the square paper.

2 To make the wings, follow steps 1 to 6 for the leaf (see page 82) using the rectangular paper.

ASSEMBLING THE BROOCH

1 Pierce the peak of the angel's body from inside using a beading awl or needle. Apply a generous amount of epoxy glue to the loop of the eye pin, insert it through the hole and pull the loop of the pin to the peak of the angel's body.

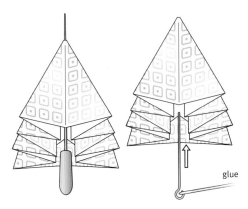

glue

glue

glue

2 Using the tip of a toothpick, apply epoxy glue between the flaps and press them together until the glue dries.

glue

3 Pierce the centre of the wing using a beading awl.

4 Insert the eye pin through the hole in the wing. Use the tip of a toothpick to apply a little epoxy glue between the angel's body and wing, then open up the wings. Coat the piece and let it dry completely.

glue

5 Thread a small bead and then a round bead on the end of the eye pin, and trim the pin, leaving 1.5 cm (1/2 in.) exposed.

6 Using round-nose pliers, bend the exposed portion of the eye pin toward the back of the angel, and make a round loop at the end of the eye pin. Connect this loop to the eye of the toggle clasp ring.

glue

7 Position the ring on top of the round bead and apply a little epoxy glue for extra strength.

8 Cut a triangular piece of plastic sheet slightly smaller than the angel. Use epoxy glue to attach it to the back of the angel, then glue the stick pin on the plastic.

ASSEMBLING THE EARRINGS

1 Follow steps 1 to 4 for the pin. Make two pieces. Thread a round bead, then glue a split ring on top of the bead.

2 Trim the pin, leaving 1 cm (3/8 in.) exposed. Use round-nose pliers to bend the exposed eye pin into a right angle, then roll it into a round loop. Attach an earring finding.

Heart earrings

Skill level: ❖ ❖

The preliminary base is enhanced to create a three-dimensional heart, which can be embellished with your favourite beads to become a must for Valentine's Day.

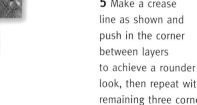

YOU WILL NEED

+ 3 cm (1¼ in.) squares yuzen washi paper (x 2)
+ 6 seed beads
+ 2 heart-shape beads
+ 4 cm (1½ in.) head pins (x 2)
+ 2 fish-hook earring findings

+ glue stick
+ epoxy glue
+ coating material and brush
+ round toothpick to apply glue
+ scissors
+ cutting pliers
+ beading awl
+ round-nose pliers

FOLDING THE HEART

1 Begin with a preliminary base (see page 20). Unfold the piece.

2 Fold all four corners to the centre, then unfold.

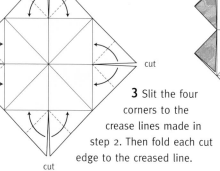

3 Slit the four corners to the crease lines made in step 2. Then fold each cut edge to the creased line.

cut

4 Refold the piece back into the preliminary base.

5 Make a crease line as shown and push in the corner between layers to achieve a rounder look, then repeat with the remaining three corners.

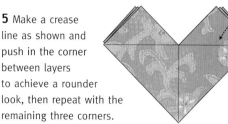

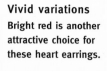

Vivid variations
Bright red is another attractive choice for these heart earrings.

6 The heart is complete and ready to be turned into an earring.

ASSEMBLING THE EARRINGS

1 Make two pieces. Complete to the end of step 3 of folding, then unfold the piece and apply glue stick to the areas shown. Complete the folding.

2 Apply epoxy glue to close the openings on the top of the heart. Pinch the piece closed until the glue dries. Coat the hearts and let them dry completely.

3 Pierce the centre of the heart with a beading awl from the bottom. Thread a seed bead on a head pin and insert it in the heart from the bottom. Thread a seed bead, a heart-shaped bead and another seed bead on the top of the pin. Cut the pin, leaving 1 cm (3/8 in.) exposed.

4 Use round-nose pliers to bend the exposed portion of pin into a right angle, then roll the bent portion into a loop. Attach earring findings.

Alternate paper, colour and beads to create your own unique Valentine heart.

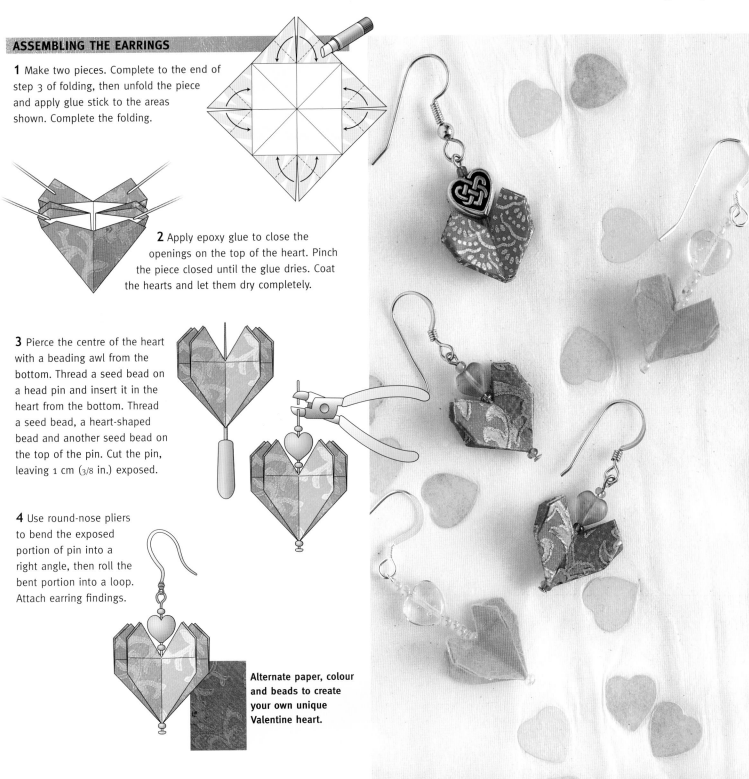

Paper crane brooch, tie tack and earrings

Skill level:

brooch ❖ ❖

tie tack ❖ ❖

earrings ❖ ❖ ❖

Traditionally a symbol of happiness, longevity, health, good luck and fortune, in recent years the crane has also become a symbol for world peace. An old tradition says that if you make a thousand cranes, your wish will come true.

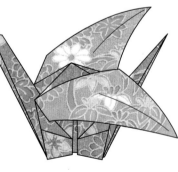

YOU WILL NEED

Brooch

+ 8.25 cm (3¼ in.) square yuzen washi paper
+ round toothpick
+ 4 x 2 cm (1½ x ¾ in.) plastic sheet
+ 2.5 cm (1 in.) bar pin

Tie tack

+ 5 cm (2 in.) square yuzen washi paper
+ round toothpick
+ 2.5 x 2 cm (1 x ¾ in.) plastic sheet
+ tie tack
+ tie tack clutch

Earrings

+ 4 cm (1½ in.) square yuzen washi paper (x 2)
+ 2 Swarovski beads
+ 4 seed beads
+ 2.5 cm (1 in.) eye pin (x 2)
+ 2 fish-hook earring findings

+ glue stick
+ epoxy glue
+ coating material and brush
+ toothpick to apply glue
+ scissors
+ beading awl
+ round-nose pliers
+ cutting pliers

FOLDING THE CRANE

1 Begin with a bird base (see page 24).

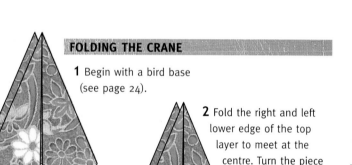

2 Fold the right and left lower edge of the top layer to meet at the centre. Turn the piece over and repeat this step on the other side.

3 Make inside reverse folds on both sides.

4 To form the crane's beak, make an inside reverse fold on one end. Pull the wings apart to complete the crane.

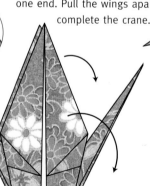

CONTINUED ON NEXT PAGE ▶

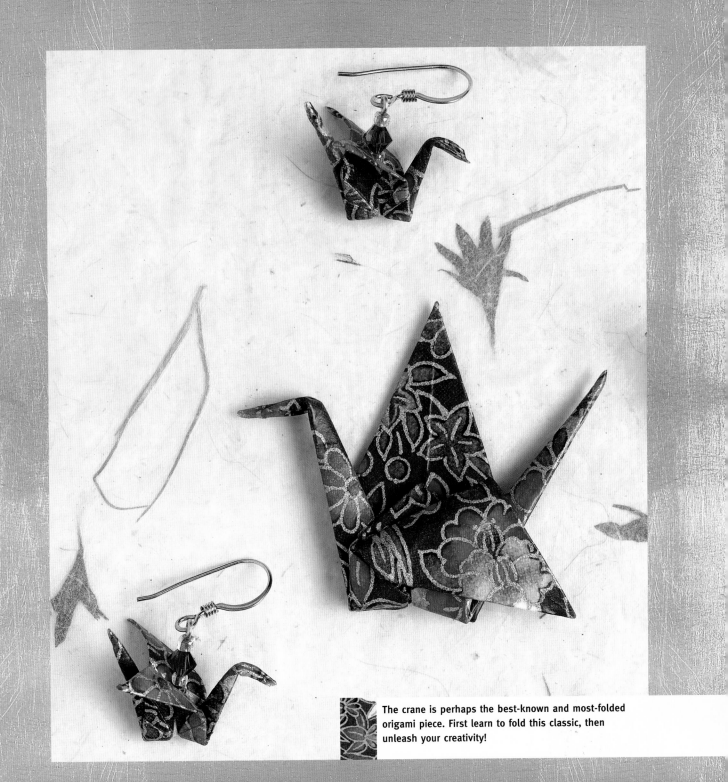

The crane is perhaps the best-known and most-folded origami piece. First learn to fold this classic, then unleash your creativity!

ASSEMBLING THE BROOCH

1 After making a bird base, open the top portion. Using a glue stick, apply glue inside (where the crane's wings will be) and then close the fold. Turn the piece over and do the same on the other side. Complete the folding to step 3.

glue

2 Fold down one wing at an angle. Make an inside reverse fold to form a crane's beak.

3 Cut a round toothpick to 1.25 cm (1/2 in.) long. Lift the wing. Apply some epoxy glue around the fold line, place the toothpick immediately beneath the fold line, and fold down the wing. This prevents the wing from being folded flat, and keeps it in place. Coat the piece and let dry completely.

4 Cut a piece of plastic sheet to the shape of the back of the crane, but slightly smaller. Using epoxy glue, glue the plastic on the back of the crane, then glue a bar pin on the plastic.

ASSEMBLING THE TIE TACK

1 Follow steps 1 to 3 for finishing the brooch. Pull back one wing and pierce it behind the crane's body with a beading awl.

2 Cut a piece of plastic to the shape of the piece (as shown) but slightly smaller. Pierce the plastic in the same position as the hole through the wing.

3 Insert a tuck pin through the hole in the wing. Apply epoxy glue to secure the pin, making sure the pin head will be hidden behind the triangular section of the crane's body.

4 With epoxy glue, attach the plastic sheet to the back of the piece, fixing the pin through the hole.

ASSEMBLING THE EARRINGS

Make two cranes and follow step 1 for the brooch. Complete the folding, then coat the pieces, and let them dry completely.

1 Pierce the centre of the crane with a beading awl, from a little hole at the bottom up to the peak of the body.

5 mm
(1/4 in)

2 Thread a seed bead, a Swarovski bead, then a seed bead on an eye pin. Insert the eye pin through the hole from the top. Trim off the bottom of the eye pin, leaving about 5 mm (1/4 in.) exposed.

3 Use round-nose pliers to bend the bottom of the eye pin, and tuck it in the crane's tail. Using the tip of a toothpick, apply a small amount of epoxy glue to the tail.

4 Press the crane tail closed with fingers (or a clip) and secure the eye pin. Hold until the glue dries.

5 Attach findings to complete. Make a second earring in the same way.

Vivid variations
The dazzling palettes of colours available for origami paper enable you to create beautifully colourful variations.

Kimono brooch and earrings

Skill level: ❖ ❖

The kimono, a traditional Japanese garment, is a straight-line and full-length robe with very wide sleeves. It is wrapped tightly around the body by the obi (sash), and secured by the obijime (sash band). It may not be the most practical garment, but it is surely one of the most beautiful. When wearing a kimono, the left side always goes over the right. Select paper for the kimono and obi as you would a dress for a doll.

YOU WILL NEED

Brooch

+ 4.5 x 17.75 cm (1¾ x 7 in.) yuzen washi paper for the kimono
+ 4 x 2.5 cm (1½ x 1 in.) yuzen washi paper for the obi
+ about 15 cm (6 in.) length knotting cord
+ polyester stuffing
+ 4 cm (1½ in.) square plastic sheet
+ 2.5 cm (1 in.) bar pin

Earrings

+ 2.5 x 10 cm (1 x 4 in.) yuzen washi paper for the kimono (x 2)
+ 2.5 x 1.25 cm (1 x ½ in.) yuzen washi paper for the obi (x 2)
+ about 7.5 cm (3 in.) length knotting cord (x 2)
+ 2 wood beads
+ 2 fish-hook earring findings

+ glue stick
+ epoxy glue
+ coating material and brush
+ toothpick to apply glue
+ scissors

With its kimono-inspired patterns, yuzen washi paper makes the most traditional-looking pieces. The "Fuji-musubi" (wisteria knot) used here is one of the most common ways to tie the obijime.

FOLDING THE KIMONO

1 Fold the paper for the kimono in half lengthways. Fold down the top edge of the top layer by about 1.25 cm (1/2 in.) for the brooch or about 5 mm (1/4 in.) for earrings.

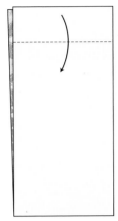

2 Mountain-fold the top edge of the top layer a little.

4 Fold the left corner down at an angle, a short way from the centre at the top, so that the corner crosses the centre crease a little. Do the same with the right corner.

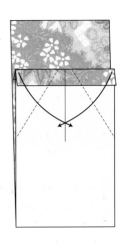

▲ **3** Fold the top layer in half widthways to mark the centre and unfold – it does not have to be creased all the way down.

5 Fold the left side of the top layer, two-thirds of the way across, then flatten the bottom to form a triangle.

6 Repeat the previous step on the right side.

7 Make mountain folds at the tops of the triangles. Turn the piece over.

8 Make a narrow fold down both sides and fold in half lengthways.

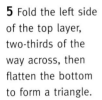

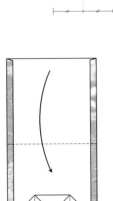

9 Turn the piece over.

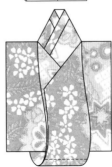

10 Align the shoulders with the tops of the sleeves. Flatten the bottom of the kimono, which is now completed.

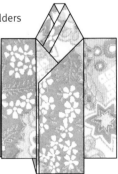

CONTINUED ON NEXT PAGE ▶

ASSEMBLING THE BROOCH

1 Follow the instructions for folding the kimono to step 8, using glue stick to stick down the narrow side folds. Continue folding the kimono to step 10.

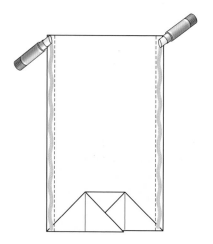

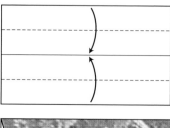

◄ 2 Open up the kimono and push stuffing inside it. Apply epoxy glue on the inside, as shown, and close the kimono.

fiberfill

◄ 3 Make the obi (sash) by folding both the top and bottom edges to meet at the centre.

▼ 4 Make the obijime (see opposite). Stick the obi around the kimono with epoxy glue. Wrap the obijime around the obi, and glue its end behind the kimono. Then glue the back of the kimono onto the sleeves.

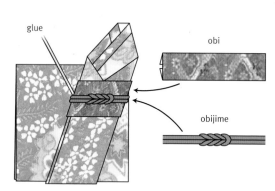

glue

obi

obijime

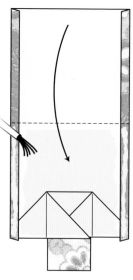

▲ 5 Turn the kimono over. Apply epoxy glue inside the sleeves and glue them together. Coat the piece and let dry completely.

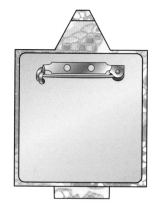

◄ 6 To complete the kimono brooch, cut a piece of plastic sheet slightly smaller than the kimono. Using epoxy glue, attach it to the back of the kimono, then glue a bar pin on the plastic.

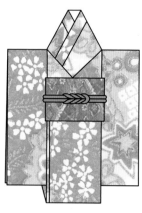

MAKING THE OBIJIME

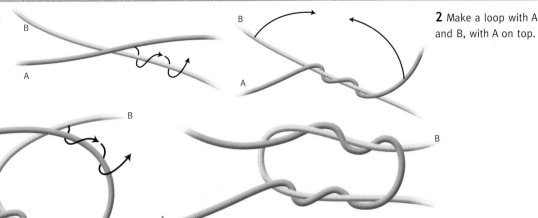

1 Cut the knotting cord into two equal lengths: cord A and cord B. Cross cord A and B, with A on top. Wrap A around B twice.

2 Make a loop with A and B, with A on top.

3 Wrap B around A twice.

4 Hold both ends of A together, and both ends of B together. Pull them gently to tie the knot.

ASSEMBLING THE EARRINGS

Make two kimonos, following steps 1 and 3 for the brooch (skip step 2).

1 Using epoxy glue, attach the obi around the kimono body and then fix the back of the kimono on the sleeves. Coat the kimonos and let dry completely.

2 Insert the cord through the loop of a fish-hook earring finding. Make a single knot. Insert both ends of the cord through a wood bead, and make another single knot.

3 Cut both ends of the cord leaving 2.5 cm (1 in.) exposed. Glue the ends of the cord inside the sleeves, leaving about 2 cm (3/4 in.) from the bead to the top of the sleeves. Glue the sleeves closed with epoxy glue.

4 Make two completed earrings.

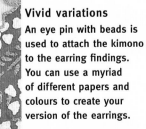

Vivid variations
An eye pin with beads is used to attach the kimono to the earring findings. You can use a myriad of different papers and colours to create your version of the earrings.

Paper fan brooch and earrings

Skill level: ❖

The Japanese paper fan, or sensu, is inspired by the shape of a bird's wing. A staple of hot-weather daily life, the sensu is also an essential part of the Japanese traditional performance arts of noh, mask drama and buyo, Japanese classic dance. Often printed, or painted, with beautiful designs, the fan brings a cool breeze to a hot, stifling day; in another context, it may be used to represent the passing of decades in the hands of a skilful noh actor.

YOU WILL NEED

Brooch
- 10 x 7.5 cm (4 x 3 in.) yuzen washi paper
- knotting cord
  7.5 cm (3 in.) length
  12.5 cm (5 in.) length
- beading or sewing thread
- 6.5 x 2.5 cm (2½ x 1 in.) plastic sheet
- 4 cm (1½ in.) bar pin

Earrings
- 7.5 x 5.5 cm (3 x 2¼ in.) yuzen washi paper (x 2)
- knotting cord
  2.5 cm (1 in.) length (x 2)
  9 cm (3½ in.) length (x 2)

- beading or sewing thread
- 1½ x 1 in. (4 x 2.5 cm) plastic sheet (x 2)
- 8 mm (5/16 in.) earring post (x 2)
- 2 earring nuts

- glue stick
- epoxy glue
- coating material and brush
- toothpick to apply glue
- scissors
- beading awl

FOLDING THE FAN

1 Fold in half lengthways to make centre crease, then unfold.

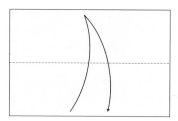

2 Fold the top edge to the centre crease and mountain-fold the bottom edge to the centre crease.

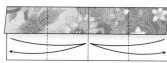
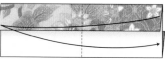

3 Fold in half widthways to make a centre crease, then unfold.

4 Fold both sides to meet at the centre crease, then unfold.

5 Fold A–A1 to meet B–B1 and unfold, then to D–D1 and unfold. Fold E–E1 to meet D–D1 and unfold, then to B–B1 and unfold.

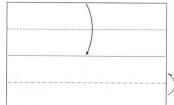
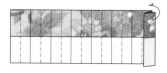

6 From one end, keep making pleats, folding in half between the creased lines you made in steps 3, 4 and 5.

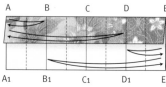

7 Flatten the piece, and tie the centre of the bottom part with thread.

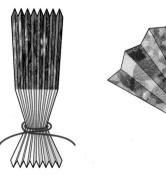

8 Open up the top and bottom pleats to form a fan.

ASSEMBLING THE BROOCH

1 Follow the steps for folding the fan, using a glue stick to apply glue when folding the bottom and top edges to the centre in step 2. Leave the glue to dry before completing the folding. Coat the piece and let dry completely.

2 Make a bow with the longer length of knotting cord, and set it aside. Twist the shorter cord twice around the point where the fan is tied, then use epoxy glue to stick the ends on the back. Glue the bow to the front.

3 Cut a piece of plastic sheet to the same shape as, but slightly smaller than, the fan. Use epoxy glue to stick it to the back of the fan, then glue the bar pin on the plastic. The completed fan brooch is simple and elegant.

ASSEMBLING THE EARRINGS

Make two fans, following steps 1 and 2 for the brooch.

1 Cut a plastic sheet into the same shape as, but slightly smaller than, the fan. Using epoxy glue, glue an earring post on the back of the fan, just above the point where it is tied with cord.

2 Use a beading awl to pierce the plastic to match the centre of the earring post.

3 Insert the earring post through the hole and glue the plastic to the back of the fan. Attach an earring nut to finish.

Yuzen washi adds a traditional touch, as well as richness and depth, to the sensu (fan).

Samurai helmet brooch and earrings

Skill level: ❖

In the middle ages, Japan was a nation of feuding warlords. The kabuto was the helmet worn by samurai, the Japanese warrior class, as they marched into battle protecting their masters, or tono. Each kabuto carries the distinctive insignia of the samurai's warrior clan. In modern Japan, the kabuto is used as a decoration during Boys' Festival (May 5th), when the wish is that each boy in the family will grow healthy and strong.

YOU WILL NEED

Brooch

+ 7.5 cm (3 in.) square yuzen washi paper
+ 7.5 cm (3 in.) square gold paper
+ about 25 cm (10 in.) length knotting cord
+ 4 cm (1½ in.) plastic disc or 4.5 x 2.5 cm (1¾ x 1 in.) plastic sheet
+ 4 cm (1½ in.) bar pin

Earrings

+ 4 cm (1½ in.) square yuzen washi paper (x 2)
+ 4 cm (1½ in.) square gold paper (x 2)
+ 4 seed beads
+ 2 pewter beads
+ 2.5 cm (1 in.) eye pin (x 2)
+ 2 fish-hook earring findings

+ glue stick
+ epoxy glue
+ coating material and brush
+ toothpick to apply glue
+ scissors
+ clear nail polish
+ beading awl or needle
+ round-nose pliers

A rather masculine design, the kabuto may surprise you with how well it matches your wardrobe.

FOLDING THE HELMET

Use the glue stick to glue yuzen washi and gold paper back to back. Let the glue dry completely before folding. (Tip: Use slightly larger sheets of paper. After pasting two sheets together, trim to the final size to achieve clean edges.)

1 Follow steps 1–6 of the fish brooch (see page 62).

2 To complete the helmet, fold the bottom triangle up, and insert it inside the helmet.

3 The completed helmet is now ready for finishing as a brooch or earrings.

ASSEMBLING THE BROOCH

1 After finishing step 1 of folding the helmet, apply epoxy glue on the top layer of the bottom portion, and then complete the folding. Coat the piece and let dry completely.

2 Loop a piece of cord, tie it in a bow and trim the ends, leaving about 2 cm (3/4 in.). Cut the loop in half.

3 Glue the cut loop ends inside the helmet with epoxy glue. Apply clear nail polish to the other two ends so that they will not become loose.

glue

glue

4 Cut a piece of plastic sheet to the same shape as, but slightly smaller than, the helmet. Using epoxy glue, fix the plastic to the back of the helmet, then glue a bar pin to the plastic.

5 The bow hangs down from the helmet.

ASSEMBLING THE EARRINGS

Make two helmets and follow step 1 for the brooch.

1 Pierce the top of the helmet with a beading awl or needle, pushing it through from the inside.

2 Insert an eye pin from the bottom, apply some epoxy glue on the loop of the eye pin, and pull it up out of the top of the helmet. Let the glue dry inside the helmet.

3 Slide a seed bead, a pewter bead, then another seed bead on the eye pin. Cut the eye pin, leaving 1 cm (3/8 in.) exposed.

4 Use round-nose pliers to bend the exposed end of the eye pin at a right angle to the bead, then roll it to form a loop.

5 Attach an earring finding to finish.

Frog brooch and earrings

Skill level: ❖ ❖ ❖

The Japanese word for frog, kaeru, sounds the same as the word meaning "return". The frog represents the return of good luck, health, money, loved ones and so on. Just as in western fairytales the frog is transformed into a handsome prince when kissed by the princess, the Japanese frog is also associated with spells and magic. Cast your own spell with these delightful origami frogs.

YOU WILL NEED

Brooch

- ✦ 9 cm (3½ in.) square yuzen washi paper
- ✦ 2.5 x 2 cm (1 x ¾ in.) plastic sheet
- ✦ 2.5 cm (1 in.) bar pin
- ✦ polyester stuffing

Earrings

- ✦ 5 cm (2 in.) square yuzen washi paper (x 2)
- ✦ 4 seed beads in colour A
- ✦ 4 seed beads in colour B
- ✦ 4 cm (1½ in.) eye pin (x 2)
- ✦ 2 fish-hook earring findings
- ✦ polyester stuffing

- ✦ glue stick
- ✦ epoxy glue
- ✦ coating material and brush
- ✦ toothpick to apply glue
- ✦ scissors
- ✦ beading awl
- ✦ round-nose pliers
- ✦ cutting pliers

FOLDING THE FROG

1 Follow steps 1–9 of the crab brooch (see page 74). Make inside reverse folds on both sides, to bring legs all the way up.

2 Turn the piece over.

3 Fold one flap to the side to show the face with a triangle flap.

4 Make inside reverse folds on both sides, bringing the legs horizontal.

5 Make inside reverse folds on all four legs, to form joints.

6 Make inside reverse folds at the tips of all four legs, as indicated by the dotted lines.

7 The completed frog is ready to leap!

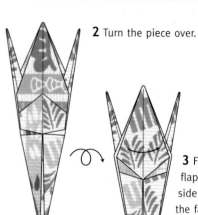

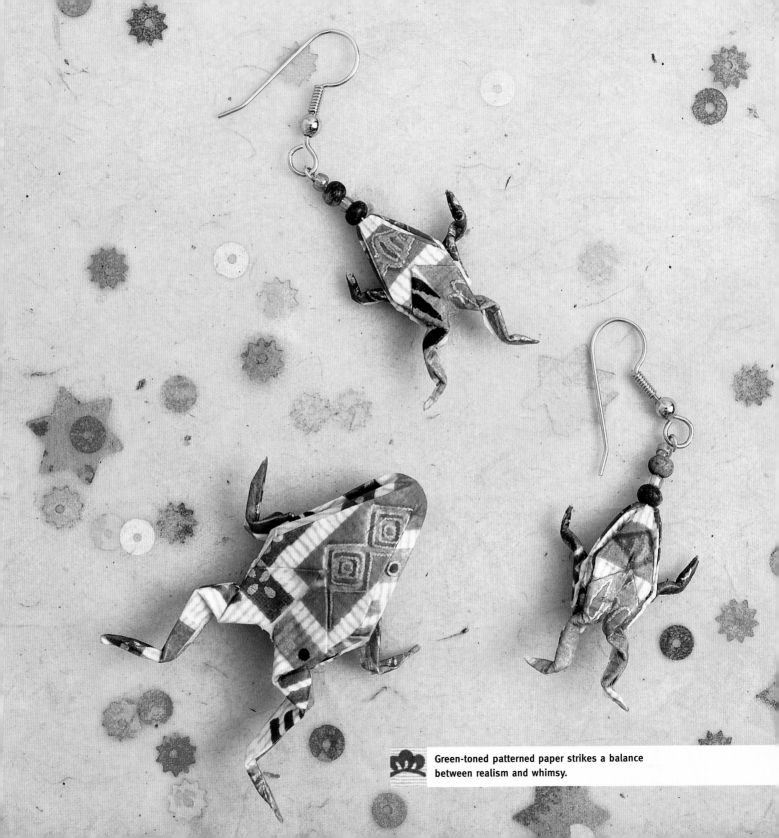

Green-toned patterned paper strikes a balance between realism and whimsy.

ASSEMBLING THE BROOCH

1 Follow the instructions for folding the frog as far as step 5 of folding the crab, then open the triangular flaps and use a glue stick to apply glue to the inside. Complete the folding.

2 Insert stuffing inside the frog, pushing it in through the small hole on the bottom using a blunt toothpick. (A sharp, or pointed, toothpick will penetrate the stuffing, making it difficult to stuff the frog.)

stuffing

3 Apply small amounts of epoxy glue between layers A to E as shown, on both right and left sides of the frog. Press the glued sections together with fingers, or a clip, until the glue dries. Coat the frog and let dry completely.

glue

A
B
C
D
E

4 Cut a piece of plastic sheet to the same shape as, but slightly smaller than, the frog's body. Using epoxy glue, fix it on the back of the frog, then glue a bar pin on the plastic.

5 Turn the completed frog over.

ASSEMBLING THE EARRINGS

Make two frogs and follow steps 1 and 2 for the brooch.

1 Apply small amounts of epoxy glue between layers, as shown in step 3 for the brooch, leaving area D on one side of the frog unglued. Press the glued sections together with fingers or clip until the glue dries. Coat the frogs and let dry completely.

A
B
C
D
E

glue

2 Use a beading awl or needle to pierce the frog through the centre, from the small hole on the bottom up to the top of the body.

3 Thread seed beads in colour A, B, A and then B on an eye pin. Insert the eye pin from the top, down through the hole in the frog. Cut the bottom of the eye pin, leaving about 5 mm (1/4 in.) exposed.

4 Use the round-nose pliers to bend the bottom of the eye pin, and tuck it in the unglued area from step 1; apply glue and secure the eye pin.

5 Attach earring findings to complete, then make a matching earring.

Combine the frog with large leaf-shaped beads
for an adventurous, dramatic design.

Choosing paper: see pages 12–13

Resources

ORIGAMI SOCIETIES

The following societies offer various information on the art of origami, including origami books, paper, diagrams, local groups and other origami organizations around the world.

Origami USA
www.origami-usa.org
15 West 77th Street
New York, NY 10024 USA
Tel: 212-769-5635

British Origami Society
www.britishorigami.org.uk
2a The Chestnuts
Countesthorpe
Leicester, LE8 5TL
England

Paperfolders Around the Lower Mainland (PALM)
www.origami.vancouver.bc.ca

Nippon Origami Association
www.origami-noa.com
2-064, Domir-Gobancho
12 Gobancho
Chiyoda-ku, Tokyo
102-0076 Japan

SUPPLIERS

Many art and craft supply shops stock jewellery findings, beads, glue, coating materials and assorted paper. Origami and washi paper are also available at oriental stores and bookstores.

www.OrigamiCraftSupply.com
Yuzen washi and other origami craft supplies.

Origami USA
www.origami-usa.org/thesource/agora.cgi
Origami, washi and American foil paper; origami books.
Mail order and online services.
Tel: 212-769-5635

Kinokuniya Bookstores
Visit www.kinokuniya.com for store locations.
Origami papers and yuzen washi paper; books.

Kate's Paperie
www.katespaperie.com
Fine handmade paper; paper products.
561 Broadway
New York, NY 10012
Tel: 212-941-9816

A.C. Moore
www.acmoore.com
Art and craft suppliers, including jewellery-making items and assorted paper. Over 100 stores in the US – visit the website for locations.

Joann
www.joann.com
Art and craft suppliers, including jewellery-making items and assorted paper. US-wide chain of stores.
Tel: 1-800-525-4951

Michael's
www.michaels.com
Art and craft suppliers, including jewellery-making items and assorted paper. US-wide chain of stores.
Tel: 1-800-642-4235

www.JewelrySupply.com
Jewellery-making suppliers, including findings, beads and tools. Online and mail order services.
Tel: 1-866-204-3235

OTHER USEFUL WEBSITES

OriCraft
www.oricraft.com
View the author's work and find out about her show and class schedule.

Joseph Wu Origami
www.origami.vancouver.bc.ca
Featuring a gallery, instructions, articles and links.

Index

Credits

First, I would like to thank Quarto for giving me the opportunity to write this book, and for ensuring it turned out so wonderfully. Their creativity and talent transformed my words and projects into this beautiful book.

I am grateful to my customers and students for making it possible for me to pursue origami as a profession. Many tell me how much they love my work; they give me the inspiration and energy to keep going. I also would like to thank my show promoters, who let me introduce my work to the public. Many thanks to Pat and Joe of PJ's Promotions – without your support since my first year, I could not have come this far.

And last, but most of all, thank you to my family and friends for your support throughout. I cannot thank enough my husband, Paul, and my sons, Bryan and Keith. Your loving, faithful support and encouragement are the backbone of my work and life. Thank you for your help and patience, allowing me the time I needed to work on this book. Paul, your wide range of knowledge and talents enable me to always count on your advice. You helped me through this, like many other journeys in our life together. Thank you!

This book is dedicated to my mother, who instilled a love of origami in my life.